Past Masters
General Editor Keith Thomas

Tocqueville

Past Masters

AQUINAS Anthony Kenny
ARISTOTLE Jonathan Barnes
AUGUSTINE Henry Chadwick
BACH Denis Arnold
FRANCIS BACON Anthony Quinton
BAYLE Elisabeth Labrousse
BENTHAM John Dinwiddy
THE BUDDHA Michael Carrithers
BURKE C. B. Macpherson
CERVANTES P. E. Russell
CLAUSEWITZ Michael Howard
COBBETT Raymond Williams
COLERIDGE Richard Holmes
DARWIN Jonathan Howard
DESCARTES Tom Sorell
DIDEROT Peter France
DISRAELI John Vincent
DURKHEIM Frank Parkin
GEORGE ELIOT Rosemary Ashton
ENGELS Terrell Carver
ERASMUS James McConica
FREUD Anthony Storr
GALILEO Stillman Drake
GIBBON J. W. Burrow
GOETHE T. J. Reed
HEGEL Peter Singer
HOBBES Richard Tuck
HOMER Jasper Griffin
HUME A. J. Ayer
JESUS Humphrey Carpenter
JOHNSON Pat Rogers

JUNG Anthony Stevens
KANT Roger Scruton
KIERKEGAARD Patrick Gardiner
LAMARCK L. J. Jordanova
LEIBNIZ G. MacDonald Ross
LOCKE John Dunn
MACHIAVELLI Quentin Skinner
MALTHUS Donald Winch
MARX Peter Singer
MENDEL Vitezslav Orel
MONTAIGNE Peter Burke
MONTESQUIEU Judith N. Shklar
THOMAS MORE Anthony Kenny
WILLIAM MORRIS Peter Stansky
MUHAMMAD Michael Cook
NEWMAN Owen Chadwick
PAINE Mark Philp
PAUL E. P. Sanders
PLATO R. M. Hare
PROUST Derwent May
RUSKIN George P. Landow
SCHILLER T. J. Reed
SHAKESPEARE Germaine Greer
ADAM SMITH D. D. Raphael
SPINOZA Roger Scruton
TOCQUEVILLE Larry Siedentop
VICO Peter Burke
VIRGIL Jasper Griffin
WITTGENSTEIN A. C. Grayling
WYCLIF Anthony Kenny

Forthcoming

JOSEPH BUTLER R. G. Frey
COPERNICUS Owen Gingerich
GODWIN Alan Ryan
KEYNES Robert Skidelsky
NIETZSCHE Michael Tanner

ROUSSEAU Robert Wokler
RUSSELL A. C. Grayling
SCHOPENHAUER Christopher Janaway
and others

Larry Siedentop

Tocqueville

Oxford   New York

OXFORD UNIVERSITY PRESS

1994

Oxford University Press, Walton Street, Oxford OX2 6DP
Oxford New York Toronto
Delhi Bombay Calcutta Madras Karachi
Kuala Lumpur Singapore Hong Kong Tokyo
Nairobi Dar es Salaam Cape Town
Melbourne Auckland Madrid
and associated companies in
Berlin Ibadan

Oxford is a trade mark of Oxford University Press

First published 1994 as an Oxford University Press paperback

British Library Cataloguing in Publication Data
Data available

Library of Congress Cataloging in Publication Data
Siedentop, Larry.
Tocqueville / L. A. Siedentop.
p.   cm.—(Past masters)
1. Tocqueville, Alexis de, 1805–1859—Contributions in political
science.   2. Democracy.   I. Title.   II. Series.
JC229.T8S54 1994   321.8—dc20   93–36218
ISBN 0–19–287690–2

1 3 5 7 9 10 8 6 4 2

Typeset by CentraCet Limited, Cambridge

Printed in Great Britain
by Biddles Ltd.
Guildford & King's Lynn

Prologue

It is often said that the most powerful rival visions of the future have been those of Karl Marx and Alexis de Tocqueville. If so, the latter seems to have carried the day. The recent widespread, though no doubt precarious, reaction against monolithic states, one-party governments and command economies would have delighted the liberal French aristocrat, who, from his first encounter with socialist ideas in the 1840s, considered them sentimental and, more important, reactionary. Tocqueville considered socialist ideas reactionary because they sought to extend what he saw as a dangerous development of the French *ancien régime*, the centralization of power.

How piquant that the most important book about modern democracy, *Democracy in America* (1835–40), should have been written by a French aristocrat! And there was perhaps a *soupçon* of aristocratic jealousy of new élites in Tocqueville's condemnation of government by bureaucrats or party *apparatchiks*. But his subtle, eloquent case for self-government and the dispersal of power has never been bettered. Little wonder that it had an extraordinary impact on contemporaries such as John Stuart Mill. For Tocqueville was by no means concerned only with power. He had a moral vision, a vision to which many of his readers have since succumbed. In Tocqueville's eyes, a truly self-governing democratic society offers a noble prospect, a goal which rises above the apparently inescapable commercialism of modern life.

The case for participating in government as a condition for a fully moral life was the case nearest Tocqueville's heart. His writings amount to an anguished protest against the excessive 'privatizing' of life and neglect of the value of citizenship. To that extent, Tocqueville offered a challenge to conventional—it is tempting to say 'bourgeois'—liberalism. But has liberalism even now risen to this challenge? Is a doctrine which often seems to restrict life to commercial activity and a private circle of friendship adequate, let alone ennobling? Tocqueville's challenge remains.

No other political thinker has explored so subtly the connection between forms of the state, different social conditions and moral dangers. Yet Tocqueville's place in the tradition of modern political thought remains surprisingly insecure. Why is that? Two reasons spring to mind. First, in contrast to the great early modern political philosophers such as Hobbes, Locke, and Rousseau, Tocqueville does not found his argument on explicit assumptions about human nature and proceed deductively from such premises. Secondly, in contrast to later nineteenth-century theorists such as Marx, Durkheim, or Weber, Tocqueville does not hold up a new science of society as his goal or introduce his works with a discourse on scientific method. Indeed, when placed beside self-styled 'scientific' thinkers, Tocqueville seems more like an artist. His writings are vivid and direct, highly charged with feeling and openly concerned to shape the reader's intentions. Even his most historical work, *The Ancien Régime and the Revolution* (1856), is at the same time an anguished criticism of the beliefs and practices which had led his contemporaries to acquiesce in Louis Napoleon's Empire.

Tocqueville's style of argument is not only pre-professional, but pre-bourgeois. His appeal to values—above all, the 'sacred' value of liberty—is almost intimate. His astonishingly successful attempt to stand back from the habits and ideas of different types of society, aristocratic and democratic, does not mean that he tries to suppress his admiration for the elegance, solidarities, and variety of character nurtured by the former. Nor does he conceal his disdain for the mediocrity of ambition fostered by the commercialism of a democratic society, even if it is more just. But there is also a purged aristocratic pride in the way Tocqueville refuses to be taken in by the aesthetic appeal of aristocratic societies. No sharper critic of the vanity, self-deception and cruelty of societies founded on privilege can be found.

Tocqueville had found a vantage-point which enabled him to analyse and judge social change in the Christian West without falling victim either to historicism or to the bogus neutrality claimed for a positivist social science. What was that vantage-point? And how did he find it? Those are the questions which, despite all the advances in Tocqueville criticism, remain central and unanswered.

This book is an attempt to answer those questions. In writing it,

I have been helped by comments from John Burrow, David East-wood, Robert Skidelsky, and Fergus Ungoed-Thomas. Needless to say, they bear no responsibility for any remaining faults.

L.A.S.

Keble College
Oxford
July 1993

Contents

Note on references

Most of the references to Tocqueville's writings are to the new edition of the *Œuvres complètes* (OC) which began to appear in 1951 under the direction of J. P. Mayer and the French National Commission for the publication of Tocqueville's works. When a tome comprises more than one volume, I have designated them a, b, or c. (Thus Tome I, volume 1 becomes Ia etc.) Many of the translations from the French are my own, though in the cases of *Democracy in America* and *The Ancien Régime and the Revolution* I have often relied on existing translations, especially those of George Lawrence (which is on the whole preferable to the original translation by Henry Reeve, even when revised by Francis Bowen) in the first case, and of Stuart Gilbert in the second. Yet I have tried to improve upon those translations when that seemed possible.

1 In the shadow of the Reign of Terror

Alexis de Tocqueville was born into an old Norman noble family shortly after the French Revolution. But at an early age he distanced himself from the prejudices of his family background. He became convinced that the era of aristocracy was over, and that a new type of society was emerging in the West—what he called a 'democratic society'. That conviction helped him to avoid the moral temptations to which many of his class succumbed in the early nineteenth century. Even as an adolescent, Tocqueville had a horror of self-deception. Those of his class who gave themselves up to illusions—particularly the illusion that the advent of democracy was something fortuitous, reversible, or even satanic—made him feel pity, if not scorn. His fears about the future were too sharp for him to believe that there was any alternative to clarity of mind and strength of purpose.

A democratic society, Tocqueville decided, had one compelling claim. It alone was consistent with the requirements of justice. But, at the same time, a democratic society carried with it serious moral and political risks which had to be faced and overcome. Identifying those risks so that they might be overcome provided a suitable, if at first glance surprising, vocation for a young French aristocrat after the Revolution. It was the subtlest form of *noblesse oblige*.

How did Tocqueville reach these conclusions? The circumstances of his early life throw light on the process, for Tocqueville was born, in 1805, into no ordinary situation. Nearly all of his family—grandparents, aunts, and cousins—had been guillotined during the Reign of Terror. His parents, the Comte and Comtesse de Tocqueville, had spent months in prison expecting the same fate. They still bore the traces. His father Hervé's hair had turned white at twenty-four, while his mother remained a nervous invalid. In the years after the fall of Robespierre, Tocqueville's parents tried to reconstruct something like their lives under the *ancien régime*. But it was a precarious undertaking. Everything around them, both the society outside the gates of the Chateau de

1

Verneuil and portraits hanging within, recalled civil war and frenzied hatred of *aristos*.

Unlike many French aristocrats, Hervé de Tocqueville had not emigrated. He was now therefore a rich man, for he had inherited the property of relatives who died under the guillotine. But wealth could not dispel the anxiety felt by members of a class which had borne the brunt of the accumulated grievances of centuries. Would there be any place or security for aristocrats in post-revolutionary France? That anxiety pressed on Alexis de Tocqueville as a child.

Go back. Look at the baby in his mother's arms; see how the outside world is first reflected in the still hazy mirror of his mind; consider the first examples that strike his attention; listen to the first words which awaken his dormant powers of thought; and finally take notice of the first struggles he has to endure. Only then will you understand the origin of the prejudices, habits and passions which are to dominate his life. The whole man is already there in the cradle. (*OC* Ia. 26)

These words from the early pages of *Democracy in America* are revealing. Tocqueville did not take the benevolence of the outside world for granted. A threat, only dimly perceived at first, shaped his temper and character. By all accounts Tocqueville as a boy was highly strung and impulsive, but vigilant. There was claustrophobia latent in him. His relish for freedom, even if it at first took the form of mere adventures and 'escapes', stands out from stories about his early years. That relish for freedom testifies to the background of anxiety.

The spectre of civil war haunted his imagination. Emerging from adolescence Tocqueville confessed that his mind had for years been dwelling on the idea of imprisonment or exile.

I remember thinking of the chances of prison which . . . the last forty years have shown it is not ridiculous to prepare for in advance. I had succeeded in imagining for myself an almost agreeable idea of that fearful place. I had imagined that a man shut up with books, paper and pens, ought to be able to find means to spend the time passably. (*OC* Va. 49)

Such fears made him attentive to his surroundings. He did not want to be caught by surprise. Little wonder that as an adolescent he showed a precocious interest in that bourgeois society which had violently rejected aristocracy in France. He became adept at entering into the ideas and feelings of people in different social positions. That penchant, developed at first to ward off danger, gradually became a skill and a matter of conviction.

By his mid-teens Tocqueville deplored the isolation of the old *noblesse* from the rest of French society. His earliest letters (1821–3) reveal that he feared the pretensions of the nobles would lead them into another catastrophe. The fall of Napoleon and the Bourbon Restoration had led many former *émigrés* to seek to restore the privileges of their class. At sixteen, when he entered the Royal College of Metz for his first formal schooling, Tocqueville discovered the extent of bourgeois suspicion of his class. He went out of his way to befriend a pupil from a modest background, Eugène Stoffels. Evidently Tocqueville felt a need to connect with the rest of French society.

That need to connect soon took on an ideal form. For as the young Tocqueville learned about his family history, he found the making of a myth—the story of his great-grandfather, Lamoignon de Malesherbes. From a leading family of the *noblesse de robe*, Malesherbes had been one of the boldest reformers in pre-revolutionary France. When still a young man he had succeeded his father as hereditary head of the *Cour des Aides*, and used the Court in the 1760s to denounce the 'despotism' of the royal administration.

Malesherbes' attitude owed something to attacks made a few decades earlier by Montesquieu and Boulainvilliers, during the 'nobles' reaction' against the bureaucratic state created by Richelieu and Louis XIV. But there was a difference. Malesherbes sympathized with the *philosophes'* language of 'natural equality', and from it drew new conclusions about government. By the 1770s, when the *Cour des Aides* was dissolved, Malesherbes argued not just for restoring traditional limits on royal power, but for popular self-government. His Remonstrance to Louis XVI in 1775 became one of his great-grandson's favourite texts:

Each body and each community of citizens retains the right to administer its own affairs, a right which we do not assert to be part of the primitive constitution of the Kingdom for it dates back further: it is a right of nature and of reason. Nevertheless it has been taken away from your subjects, Sire, and we are not afraid to say that in this respect the administration has fallen into childish excesses.

Ever since powerful ministers have made it a political principle not to

3

allow a national assembly to be convoked, precedent has followed precedent until it now comes about that the deliberations of villagers may be declared null, if they have not been authorized by the Intendant.   (*OC* Ia. 447)

With such arguments Malesherbes moved decisively beyond the enlightened despotism espoused by many *philosophes*. In 1774 he joined Turgot's reforming ministry, but resigned when opposition from courtiers frustrated its efforts. He spent the last years of the *ancien régime* in self-imposed exile, writing on behalf of causes such as Protestant emancipation and the legalizing of divorce.

It was Malesherbes' conduct after 1789 that completed his hold over the young Tocqueville's imagination. In 1793, Malesherbes volunteered to defend the hapless Louis XVI before the Revolutionary Convention. He thus set in motion a chain of events which led to his own death and to that of nearly all of his family. (In the same year, Malesherbes' granddaughter Louise married Hervé de Tocqueville, scion of a family of provincial Norman nobility. They survived only because Robespierre fell a few days before the date set for their execution.) The disinterestedness of Malesherbes' action in defending the King, after having been the leading critic of royal despotism, aroused an enthusiasm in his great-grandson which he never outgrew. 'I am the grandson of M. de Malesherbes: Malesherbes defended the people before the King, and the King before the people', Tocqueville wrote on a paper found after his death. 'His is a double example which I have not forgotten, and shall never forget.'

Tocqueville developed an idea of 'true' aristocracy which had more to do with quality of motives than with prejudices of caste. His cousin, Louis de Kergolay, shared his dreams. In their early teens they dreamed of the French nobility becoming leaders of the people instead of their enemies—fighting for common rights and limiting the power of the Crown, as, they were told, the English aristocracy had succeeded in doing. Probably that is why Tocqueville longed to visit England and see those 'rascally' English.

Tocqueville's early education had been confided to a gentle, witty old priest, the Abbé Lesueur. In the Abbé Tocqueville found a surrogate mother, for the Comtesse of Tocqueville was a difficult and remote invalid. The Abbé and Tocqueville became very close.

The Abbé allowed the boy remarkable freedom, encouraged his literary tastes, and nourished in him an ardent religious faith. They talked together about everything. With the Abbé, Tocqueville developed a taste for the unreserved sharing of ideas and feelings which shaped his later idea of friendship. 'Friendship, dear Louis, is all that is worth having here on earth', he wrote to Kergolay. 'The taste which I have had of other emotions has gradually convinced me of this' (*OC* XIIIa. 143).

In 1819–20 Tocqueville left Lesueur's charge in Paris to live with his father, who had become Prefect of Metz. Often left to his own devices, he began to read widely in the prefecture library. But reading the eighteenth-century *philosophes* soon put an end to his uncritical faith. The closeness of his relations with the Abbé made this crisis of faith more disturbing. It jeopardized their intimacy, and threw the sixteen-year-old Tocqueville into a state of despair from which he never fully recovered.

My life until then had developed in a setting full of faith, which hadn't even allowed doubt to touch my soul. Then doubt entered, or rather thrust itself in with unheard of violence, not merely the doubt of this or that, but universal doubt. I experienced suddenly the sensation described by those who have witnessed an earthquake, when the earth was trembling beneath them, the walls around them, the ceiling above their heads, the furniture around them, and the whole of nature before their eyes. I was seized by the blackest melancholy. (*OC* XVb. 315)

To an unusual extent, Tocqueville had a need for certainty. 'I consider doubt one of the greatest miseries of our nature; I put it immediately after illness and death'.

Could anything be salvaged from the wreck? Tocqueville's life in the 1820s became an attempt to save a few articles of faith and place them in a more intellectually compelling framework. Perhaps as a gesture to the memory of Malesherbes, he decided to study law in Paris, despite efforts by his cousin Louis (abetted by other relations descended from the military nobility) to persuade him to join the army. The Abbé Lesueur opposed that idea. He perceived the quality of his young charge's mind, and did everything he could to stimulate literary ambition in Tocqueville.

Tocqueville could hardly have chosen a better moment to study in Paris. By 1822–3 a 'Great Debate' was under way in the

Chambers and in the press. The relatively liberal governments of the early Restoration had given way, after the assassination of the heir to the throne in 1820, to an ultra-royalist ministry dominated by Villèle. In the mid-1820s the Villèle government introduced a series of bills which touched every aspect of society and government in France, bills which the liberal opposition interpreted as nothing less than an attempt to restore the *ancien régime*. The liberals, led by Royer-Collard, claimed the struggle was between 'the *ancien régime* and the revolution, between the old France and the new, between "aristocracy" and "democracy"'. It is clear from what he wrote just a few years later that Tocqueville followed the Great Debate closely. It provided him with the basic categories of his thought—'aristocracy' and 'democracy', 'atomization' and 'centralization'. It inculcated the habit of comparing two types of society. The Great Debate created a binocular vision in Tocqueville which he never lost.

By 1827–8 Tocqueville was well on his way to becoming a liberal. A journal he kept when travelling through Italy with his brother Edouard, after completing his legal studies, exudes enthusiasm for civil and political liberty. He is scathing about the Neapolitan aristocracy for lending themselves to royal tyranny rather than championing popular rights. Tocqueville also became a member of the *Society for Christian Morality*, a liberal pressure group dominated by the historian François Guizot. The ideas put forward by this group reveal the strong Protestant influence on Restoration liberalism. Guizot, like Madame de Staël and Benjamin Constant, argued that liberalism, far from being a threat to Christianity, as supposed by Catholic royalists, should be understood as applied Christianity. For liberalism, like Christianity itself, rested on the assumption of moral equality and held that morality could only issue from conscience or uncoerced choice, the ultimate justification for civil liberty.

That quasi-Protestant interpretation allowed Tocqueville to save 'Christian morality', a concept which looms large in his later writings, from the wreck of his faith. That interpretation helped him towards a new credo. Henceforth Tocqueville invested 'the good cause' of liberalism with the passion which simple faith had originally sustained in him. A few years later, when the critic

Saint-Beuve met him for the first time, he immediately identified Tocqueville as a 'believer'.

The study of law did not begin to satisfy Tocqueville's curiosity or ambition. He had been furthering his political education, with the help of a former teacher at Metz, by comparing the development of English and French institutions since the Middle Ages. This choice was no accident. Such comparison had become central to liberal argument during the Great Debate. England, after all, provided the model for the representative government which Restoration France had introduced. Why had England developed representative government, when France had fallen victim to absolute monarchy? The question began to haunt Tocqueville.

In 1827 he was made a junior magistrate at Versailles where his father had recently become the Prefect. But, despite his connections, his hopes of rapid advancement were disappointed. The magistracy proved a difficult vocation, lacking the excitement he almost morbidly needed. He also found public speaking an ordeal. His voice was too soft. He was too fastidious. He wanted to express his ideas exactly, but he could not improvise—in contrast to another young magistrate, Gustave de Beaumont. Beaumont, an affable young noble from the Touraine, was a confirmed liberal. Stimulated by Tocqueville's ideas, Beaumont became a protective friend. Tocqueville needed such intimacy. For he was not satisfied by the routine-bound attitudes of his colleagues. 'I am afraid that in time I may become a kind of legal machine like most of my colleagues who are so specialized that they are as incapable of judging a great movement or leading a great undertaking as they are skilful in deducing a series of axioms or in finding analogies . . .', he wrote to Kergolay. 'I would rather burn my books than reach that point' (*OC* XIIIa. 108).

In 1827 the ultra-royalist Government was defeated in elections, and gave way to the moderate Martignac ministry, widely seen as offering the last chance of compromise between the Bourbons and the liberal party in France. When the new ministry lifted the ban on university lectures, Guizot began a series of lectures on the *History of Civilization in Europe and in France*, which became a rallying-point for the young liberal intelligentsia. In his lectures Guizot exploited ideas from the Great Debate—notably, atomization and centralization—in order to give a trenchant account of the development of European institutions and beliefs. Tocqueville found Guizot's lectures compelling. 'The analytical mind of Guizot' became a model for him and for nearly three years he made the journey from Versailles to Paris every Saturday in order to join the large, excited crowds at the Old Sorbonne.

Meanwhile, lack of progress in his legal career made Tocqueville frantic. He desperately wished to make a mark in the world. Referring to this period years later, he confessed that he 'would have jumped over Notre Dame, if I had thought that what I wanted was on the other side'. But what did he want? By 1829–30 he wanted to take a leading part in establishing representative government in France as that form of government, he believed, was the only one appropriate to the moral requirements of European 'civilization' (a notion from Guizot on which he now relied). The decline of aristocracy, or what Guizot called the 'rise of the middle classes', neither could nor should be reversed. For the new democratic condition of society was alone consistent with natural justice and, behind it, Christian morality. Studies which Beaumont and he undertook were designed to prepare them for politics by giving them a deeper understanding of social and political change in Europe. The re-emergence of towns and a market economy in the later feudal period, the development of the bourgeoisie as a class together with the centralization of government, these themes provided a focus for their studies.

In 1829, Charles X dismissed Martignac and appointed the Prince de Polignac instead. The elections which followed yielded a majority hostile to Polignac, however, and thus posed starkly the issue of representative government. Determined to govern without having a ministry imposed on him, the King seemed to be inviting revolution. The crisis of 1829–30 raised again the spectre of civil war which had disturbed Tocqueville's childhood. His health suffered. Despite his youth and obscurity, Tocqueville visited leading liberals such as Guizot to discuss the crisis—he wanted *to do something*. He identified with public issues so intensely that he must have seemed priggish to the politicians he interviewed.

Revolution in July 1830 confirmed his worst fears. The attempt to re-establish aristocratic privilege in France had failed and nearly destroyed representative government with it. Tocqueville and

Beaumont decided to resist the royal *coup d'état*. While liberals in Paris proclaimed Louis-Philippe the new king, Tocqueville, who had joined the National Guard in Versailles, watched coaches carry Charles X away to exile. He was appalled by the blindness which had put off the day when the new and old élites in France might merge.

After July, Tocqueville and Beaumont found their careers compromised because, although both had opposed the royal *coup d'état*, their aristocratic backgrounds made them suspect. They also faced disapproval from legitimist relations when they swore the oath of allegiance required by the new regime. Tocqueville could no longer see his way forward. It seemed that he was doomed to remain a minor magistrate. But such an outcome was intolerable to his ambition. 'I recognize every day that I have a need to be foremost which will be the cruel torment of my life' (*OC* XIIIa. 107). Political instability made matters worse. The new regime was far from secure. Further disturbances might usher in a more radical regime, even a 'democratic republic'. Would aristocrats then be persecuted or forced into exile again?

For several years Tocqueville had toyed with the idea of visiting the United States. The debate about centralization in France first directed his attention there in the late 1820s. By 1828 he had accepted the Restoration liberals' definition of the chief political problem facing a modern democratic society. How could a balance between central power and local autonomy be found in such a society, when local autonomy was no longer guaranteed by aristocratic power? In France, the destruction of aristocracy had also brought with it the destruction of local autonomy, while the survival of local autonomy in England depended upon the dominance of an aristocracy. But now the English model was suspect.

In Tocqueville's eyes, the July Revolution established beyond doubt that attempting to recreate an aristocracy was *not* the way to limit centralization in France. He began to suspect that American institutions would provide a more helpful model for France than those of England. In America, it should be possible to observe a democratic society governing itself in a decentralized way. How had the Americans managed that? If he could explain the nature of American federalism, he might do a major service for France—

which seemed to be heading for a republic, but in which 'republic' had previously meant only a form of centralized power exercised in the name of the people. He might also lift himself from obscurity and lay the foundation for a political career. For once, self-interest and idealism pointed in the same direction.

In the autumn of 1830 Tocqueville and Beaumont began to plan for a journey to the United States. They had come up with a plausible pretext. One of the reforms being discussed in the aftermath of the July Revolution was the new 'penitentiary' system for prisoners which had been introduced in Philadelphia and Auburn, New York. With the help of influential friends, they secured permission to visit the United States to inspect the new type of prison.

Tocqueville was unquestionably the driving spirit: the far more relaxed Beaumont watched his friend with a mixture of dismay and amusement. Yet Beaumont's good humour helped to overcome the frequent bouts of depression to which Tocqueville was subject, when 'stomach troubles' reduced him to 'imbecility'. Such bouts reveal the pitch of excitement at which Tocqueville lived.

Tocqueville and Beaumont reached New York City in May 1831. They were at once struck by the unprecedented social equality, by the absence of the status differences which were the legacy of feudalism in Europe. They were also struck by the frenetic commercial activity. Social equality seemed to be tied to the dominance of the market-place and a 'profit-loss' mentality. At first Tocqueville's reaction was tinged with disdain. But as the days went by, that reaction turned into one of grudging acceptance and, finally, open admiration—especially after they left New York City for frontier regions to the West. What overcame Tocqueville's prejudices were the advantages which followed from the lack of class consciousness.

The most notable advantage was what he called 'the absence of government'. By that he meant the absence of the state machine familiar in France, the extent to which Americans were able to manage their own affairs. The vigour of civil society in America convinced Tocqueville that he had been right in looking to America for a model for reform of the French state. With his hunch vindicated, he was eager to observe as much as possible.

10

It is impossible to imagine the activity of mind and body which, like a burning fever, preyed upon him incessantly. Rest was foreign to his nature; and whether his body was actively employed or not, his mind was always at work ... The smallest loss of time was unpleasant to him. This notion kept him in a constant state of tension; and in his travels it became such a passion that he never reached a place without first assuring himself of the means of leaving it, so that one of his friends said that his departure always preceded his arrival. (*OC* [Beaumont] I. 21–3)

Beaumont could hardly keep up with him, and found relief in sketching and playing the flute.

Yet Tocqueville had a contemplative side. When they reached the Michigan wilderness the sight of endless virgin forest relaxed him as little else could do. At least momentarily he was freed from social conflicts.

When at noon the sun's rays penetrate the forest, there is often heard a long sob, a kind of plaintive cry echoing in the breeze. Deep silence ensues, and such absolute stillness as fills the mind with a kind of superstitious awe. In this flowery wilderness, where, as in Milton's paradise all seems prepared for the reception of man, the feelings produced are tranquil admiration, a soft melancholy, a vague aversion to civilized life, and a sort of savage instinct which causes you to regret that soon this enchanting solitude will be no more. (*OC* Va. 370)

The Michigan wilderness drove away the spectre of civil war which otherwise dominated his imagination.

From Michigan they travelled to Canada, where they delighted in survivals of the French *ancien régime*, and then on to Boston. By this time they had nearly completed their enquiry into the penitentiary system. It was a relief. The pretext of their journey had become a slight bore.

As the penitentiary system is supposed to be our occupation, we must, like it or not, exploit it every day. In vain do we sometimes try to elude it. Everyone finds a way of introducing some amiable allusion to prisons. At social events, the mistress of the house or her daughter—beside whom one of us is carefully placed—would think herself impolite if she did not open the conversation by speaking of hangings and floggings. (*OC* [Beaumont] VII. 71)

Tocqueville now devoted himself to the political institutions of New England and he found what he had hoped to find. The

11

autonomy of the township fostered self-reliance and the habit of association, so that Americans seemed in large part to be able to do without government. Tocqueville explored the ways in which the federal system, through constitutional rules and a new role for the courts, helped to make this possible. In New England, he discovered local officials who were held accountable by local people, rather than bureaucrats embodied in an administrative hierarchy. Little wonder that he turned the New England township into an instructive myth.

From New England the two friends set out to explore the southern states by way of Kentucky and the Mississippi valley. They nearly drowned when their steamship hit a rock in the Ohio River. Forced to travel overland in savage weather, Tocqueville fell ill and had to be nursed back to health in a log cabin in Tennessee. When at last they resumed their journey, what they saw of the southern states convinced them that slavery had created the only approximation to an aristocratic society in America.

The constant movement, novelty and danger of the journey suited Tocqueville. He had an almost morbid need of excitement. The return to France in March 1832, was therefore a dreadful anti-climax. He was plunged back into the awkward professional situation he had left behind. When Beaumont (who complained he was being 'used' by the Government) resigned from the magistracy, Tocqueville did the same. This resignation made it possible for him to devote his time to a book on American institutions, while Beaumont composed their report on the penitentiary system.

Tocqueville had meanwhile become attached to an English-woman, Mary Mottley. Mary was middle-class, rather plain and without much fortune. But her detachment from the usual French prejudices and her taste for ideas appealed to him. When they married in 1835, it was a *mésalliance* in the eyes of his family. Tocqueville, however, could not bear the arranged marriages characteristic of his class. The company of Mary had been a great personal support to him in 1833–4, when he spent most of each day in a garret writing. It was, Beaumont later observed, 'the happiest period' of Tocqueville's life.

Democracy in America was published in 1835. Its success exceeded Tocqueville's wildest hopes. Royer-Collard dubbed him the 'new Montesquieu'. While he enjoyed the change in his position, Tocqueville tried not to lose his head. (He compared himself to a woman at Napoleon's court whose husband had just been made a Duke, but who, when she heard 'the Duchess' announced, moved to one side to make way for the 'great lady'.) Stimulated by a visit to aristocratic England in the summer of 1835, and encouraged by the praise of leading Whigs and Radical thinkers such as J. S. Mill, Tocqueville decided to write a companion volume to *Democracy in America* tracing the effects of a democratic society on ideas, feelings and customs. However, the second part, in conception even more unprecedented than the first, was to take longer and give him far more trouble than he dreamed.

Tocqueville was already looking for ways of putting his new fame to use politically. Cultivating electors in at least two parts of Normandy, he failed to be elected in 1837 because he rejected support offered by the Government. The restricted suffrage, joined to the centralized form of the French state, opened the door to government manipulation of the electoral process, a practice which Tocqueville detested. However, his rejection of government support put him in a strong position two years later, when he easily won Valognes, the town nearest to his charming Norman château.

These demands on his time made the writing of the second part of *Democracy in America* a slow, uneven process, and when it finally appeared in 1840, the book did not arouse the same enthusiasm as the first part. In retrospect the novel character of his argument and its more abstract quality hardly make that surprising. Yet Tocqueville was disappointed. He had hoped for another popular success, which might both further his political career and contribute to the 'good cause' of liberal institutions in France.

Altogether, the 1840s proved to be difficult, unhappy years. Tocqueville found that he lacked skills needed for a parliamentary career, just as he had for the magistracy. Absorbed in ideas, he was not good at parliamentary tactics or dealings with his colleagues (he found it hard even to remember the names of those who had not impressed him). His soft voice made public speaking an ordeal. In a state of tension, he would spend days preparing a speech, and, when it was over, he often became unable to eat because of his nervous stomach. Conscious of superior abilities, Tocqueville wanted to achieve a leading position among his contemporaries. His failure to do so drove him nearly to despair.

He may have looked for consolation outside marriage, but that only increased his melancholy and isolation. He had always relied upon some friend to act as 'confidant' in succession to the Abbé Lesueur, first his cousin Kergolay and then Beaumont. While being reserved with others, Tocqueville opened himself to such friends to an unusual extent. Indeed, he once compared himself to a bottle with too narrow a neck—'when it was turned upside down either nothing came out or everything'. Unfortunately, in the parliamentary manœuvres of the 1840s Tocqueville's friendship with Beaumont suffered. He found himself without anyone in whom he could confide.

Beaumont and he had entered the Chamber hoping to create a truly liberal party in France, one which accepted the new democratic condition of society but did *not* accept the centralized form of the French state. Their goal was to initiate the French into self-government at every level, and gradually create free *mœurs*—that is the attitudes and habits of a free people, as distinct from their laws. Hardly had they reached the Chamber, however, when the Near Eastern Crisis of 1840–1 ushered in a ministry dominated by Guizot, who proved to be a superb manipulator of the system of limited suffrage established by the July Monarchy. There resulted a period in which French politics, dominated by narrowly bourgeois interests, utterly lacked any ideal impress. Tocqueville, who regretted the 'great issues' of Restoration politics and deplored the bourgeois *pot-au-feu* which had taken its place, found himself reduced to a Cassandra-like role which did not satisfy his desire to lead.

The February Revolution of 1848 rescued Tocqueville from that impasse. He immediately identified the threat to liberal institutions which the fear of socialism, ascendant in the Paris working class, would create. Yet, at the same time, he revelled in the excitement and in the gravity of the issues at stake. It is a paradox of Tocqueville's life that the humdrum functioning of a parliamentary system which he sought to establish in France yielded the sort of politics which failed to ignite his imagination, whereas a revolutionary situation did.

In May 1848 Tocqueville was elected by a massive majority to the new Assembly and took part in the suppression of the uprising by the Paris working class on 15 May, displaying considerable personal courage. Afterwards, his reputation led to his being named to the committee drafting a new constitution. However, he failed to carry his colleagues in measures of decentralization, while he acquiesced in the rule that the directly elected President should be permitted only one term. The dangers attending that rule became apparent by the autumn of 1848, when Prince Louis Napoleon stood for the Presidency. Tocqueville supported his unsuccessful opponent, General Cavaignac.

In 1849, after renewed rioting in Paris, Louis Napoleon appointed Tocqueville Foreign Minister. During his short tenure, he had to deal with the consequences of French intervention in the Roman Revolution and a crisis caused by revolutionaries from Russia and Austria-Hungary taking refuge in Turkey. These were not problems which permitted dramatic successes. (Indeed, Tocqueville's appointment of his ultramontane friend Corcelle as ambassador to the Papal Curia embroiled French policy, because Corcelle was unwilling to put pressure on the Pope or cardinals in favour of a liberal constitutional settlement in Rome.) Yet Tocqueville was able to take pride in his role in helping to prevent French armies outside Rome bombarding the ancient city.

Contact with Louis Napoleon both fascinated and repelled Tocqueville, who was struck by the way events masked a strain of fantasy in the new President which amounted almost to madness. Louis Napoleon, on the other hand, admired Tocqueville, and regretted losing him when he dismissed the Barrot Ministry late in 1849. By that time, however, Tocqueville and other leading politicians had no doubts about the Prince-President's goal. He wished to restore the Napoleonic Empire.

From 1849 to 1851 Tocqueville's attention was dominated by the struggle between the President and the Assembly. When he was made spokesman for the committee examining the issue, Tocqueville urged changing the rule which forbade re-election of the President. That was during the summer of 1851. Tocqueville had been obliged to spend the previous winter in Sorrento as his exertions as Foreign Minister had taken a heavy toll of his health. In March 1850 he had coughed up blood, the first symptom of the tuberculosis which eventually killed him.

Louis Napoleon's *coup d'état* on 2 December 1851 came as no surprise. Imprisoned briefly at the Quai d'Orsai, Tocqueville smuggled out a letter of protest which appeared in the London *Times*. The liberal cause for which he had struggled since the late 1820s seemed lost. But for how long? He did not delude himself. A regime founded on the army and the peasantry's fear of socialism was likely to last for some time.

Tocqueville believed that he had no choice but to abandon public life. He had already taken precautions. During the winter in Sorrento, in addition to writing his *Souvenirs* of the 1848 Revolution, he had begun to plan another book. His spell as Foreign Minister had persuaded him that he was more likely to make a mark on his generation by writing than by holding office and now, in any case, the latter option was closed. He would not serve a tyrant. The book he planned was to be more than a literary exercise, however. It was to be political action in another form. For Tocqueville decided that the origins of the First Napoleonic Empire could throw light on the Second—by showing how a revolution made in the name of liberty had resulted in military despotism. His intention was to show how class conflict continued to undermine free institutions in France.

After 1851 Tocqueville found the salons of Paris distasteful. His pride could not brook being reduced to a courtier. Anyway, Louis Napoleon was a poor facsimile of Louis XIV. Tocqueville and Mary spent more time in Normandy, visiting Paris only when he needed books to pursue his researches on the Revolution. He was soon absorbed in examining the condition of French society and the structure of its government in the decades prior to 1789. When his deteriorating health forced him to abandon the chill, damp atmosphere of Normandy for the softer climate of Tours, in 1853–4, Tocqueville was able to examine the almost complete records of a pre-Revolutionary Intendancy.

At times his spirits were sapped by despondency about the Second Empire. His life became that of an internal exile. He resisted the blandishments of Louis Napoleon to return to public life. Instead, he preferred to keep in touch with like-minded friends, with liberals still devoted to the 'good cause'. His correspondence grew enormously in the 1850s. He was in search of liberal solidarity.

Tocqueville's letters often reveal the whole man more than his books. He pruned rigorously whatever he published. But his letters have the freedom and *élan* of the moment, a finesse which picks out the mood of the recipient, and delicate humour which would not have been out of place in a salon. Tocqueville's curiosity, his civic spirit and innocent commitment to free institutions, helped him to retain a boyish enthusiasm into middle age. He had the irony of the *ancien régime* without its cynicism. Such qualities gave him a peculiar hold over his friends. When they came to stay at the château de Tocqueville he led them on long walks, talking about literature, travel, history, and, of course, politics. Becoming absorbed in some idea, Tocqueville's stride would quicken. He scarcely seemed to notice obstacles in his path.

By the mid-1850s the chief obstacle to his work was his health. Yet he managed to learn German and visit the Rhineland in order to understand something of eighteenth-century Germany. In 1856 he brought out what was intended to be only a preliminary volume, *The Ancien Régime and the Revolution*, devoted to the origins of the 1789 revolution. Would the book be a success? Tocqueville desperately wanted to strike a blow at the Second Empire. Yet he feared that the liberal assumptions which governed his argument were so out of keeping with the spirit of the times that the book might not succeed. He was wrong. *The Ancien Régime and the Revolution* became his second major success.

Throughout Europe Tocqueville was now looked upon as the leading spokesman of French liberalism. When he visited London in 1857 to inspect the British Museum collection on the French Revolution, the visit evoked a prolonged, even disconcerting, tribute by British society. He was summoned by Prince Albert for a tête-à-tête, fêted at dinners which wrought havoc on his stomach, and returned by British warship to his own Cherbourg peninsula. These tributes almost overcame Tocqueville's irritation at the way the British government had earlier shown itself so uncaring about the overthrow of political liberty in France.

If Tocqueville's curiosity had not dwindled, his strength had. In 1858 he again coughed up blood with the result that his doctor insisted that he spend the coming winter in the Mediterranean. Mary's state of mind was now a serious obstacle, however. She had never recovered her serenity after doubting Tocqueville's fidelity, despite the fact that he remained, *au fond*, devoted to her. Observing the symptoms which presaged his tubercular decline, she developed complaints as if in sympathy. For her, the prospect of life without him must have been terrible. His family had never accepted her. She remained an Englishwoman stranded in France.

Their journey south to Cannes in November 1858 was a disaster. Winter set in prematurely, and Tocqueville arrived half-dead. In the following months, the mild Provençal climate brought occasional improvements. But the outcome, as Beaumont dolefully noted, was never in doubt. Tocqueville died in April 1859, not yet fifty-four years old.

France thus lost its greatest liberal thinker—a thinker who had reconciled Montesquieu's emphasis on the dispersing of political power with an unequivocal acceptance of the democratic direction of social change, a mind which combined a modern commitment to individual autonomy with an ancient concern for civic spirit or patriotism. Much controversy has been aroused over whether or not Tocqueville died a Christian. It is perhaps most accurate to say that he was a half-believer—a believer in what he called 'Christian morality'. By that he understood belief in the natural equality and brotherhood of men, and of the right to equal liberty which results.

Tocqueville had a complaint against the Christian Church. In his eyes the Church had never drawn out the political implications of its moral beliefs. It had never made clear that government must be based on consent and the form of government such that it can mobilize consent. Nor had the Church ever proclaimed that citizens have a duty to concern themselves with public affairs. That is why Tocqueville said that his chief aim in entering politics was to reconcile Christianity and the modern world, by showing how a liberal doctrine of civic duty was needed to complete Christian morality. The Church, especially the Catholic Church, had to accept responsibility for the world it had helped to create, and sanction the free institutions which fulfilled it.

Liberty was not something Tocqueville took lightly. His large, fine, sad eyes—which dominate the portraits—bespeak its heavy responsibilities. Two years before his death, he wrote to his oldest friend:

You know that one of my first opinions is that life has no period of rest; that external and, still more, internal exertion is as necessary in age as in youth—no, even more necessary. Man is a traveller towards a colder and colder region, and the higher his latitude, the faster ought to be his walk. *The great malady of the soul is cold.* In order to combat this formidable evil, it is necessary not only to keep one's mind active through work, but through contact with other men and with the affairs of this world. It is especially at this age that one cannot survive on what one has already learned but must attempt to learn more.   (*OC* XIIIb. 324–5)

Tocqueville had come into the world against a sombre background. It is hardly surprising that his life was so restless and intense.

2 The Great Debate of the 1820s

During the 1820s Tocqueville led a double life. His outer life was that of a law student and, after 1827, a very junior magistrate at Versailles. It was a life marked more by frustration than by success. For he found the study of law tedious, while diffidence about public speaking prevented him achieving any promotion as a magistrate. Tocqueville's inner life was another story, however. During these years he had an intellectual adventure of the first order. The excitement which his career denied him was provided by a framework of ideas he constructed for himself, drawing on the Great Debate of the 1820s. That framework of ideas gradually drew his attention to the United States, and led him to invest American institutions with a significance previously unrecognized.

Strangely, the importance of these years for Tocqueville's development has been overlooked, perhaps because Tocqueville left behind no account of his own intellectual formation. Moreover, when writing *Democracy in America* (1835), he sought a novelty which did not lead him to emphasize his debts. His remark that when writing about a subject he preferred *not* to read other books about it, and his confession that it was only after 1835 that he first read political philosophers such as Plato and Machiavelli, have also misled. Such things have drawn attention away from his apprenticeship in the 1820s.

Yet whenever letters allow us to glimpse Tocqueville in the 1820s, he is immersed in study. In 1825, with the help of a former teacher at Metz, he began to compare the historical development of French and English institutions, at the moment when that comparison had become central to liberal argument in the Great Debate. In the later 1820s, he pursued another ambitious programme of study with his new friend Beaumont, and once again writings by liberals such as Guizot and Barante were central. The works Tocqueville read were mostly historical. But it was history with a difference—analytical or sociological history which drew heavily on liberal argument in the Great Debate. It contained a great deal of social and political theory.

The debates of Restoration politics were thus the catalyst for Tocqueville's ideas. The evidence, both direct and indirect, is that writings by liberals known as the *Doctrinaires*—Royer-Collard, Barante, and Guizot—as well as by Madame de Staël and Benjamin Constant shaped his mind. Tocqueville's encomium to his grandfather Malesherbes—'who defended the people before the King, and the King before the people'—was taken from Madame de Staël's *Reflections on the French Revolution* (1818), a work which set the scene for liberal argument in the next decade.

We know from Tocqueville's letters that he attended lectures by François Guizot for more than two years until the Revolution of 1830. He also devoured Guizot's writings, and held up his analytical approach as exemplary. In August 1829 he wrote to Beaumont:

We must reread [Guizot's *History of Civilization*] together this winter, my dear friend. It is prodigious in its analysis of ideas and choice of words, truly prodigious. Reading it has given me a considerable insight into the fourth century, which was previously totally unknown to me and which has, however, all the interest the decomposition of the great Roman machine can offer. (*OC* VIIIa. 80–1)

Equally striking was Tocqueville's veneration for Pierre Royer-Collard, who led the liberal opposition to the ultra-royalist government in the 1820s and sought a *modus vivendi* between the Bourbons and the liberals. No other statesman ever won such approval from Tocqueville. When publication of *Democracy in America* made him famous, Tocqueville immediately seized the chance to cultivate Royer-Collard's friendship, treating him as his mentor and almost a father figure—stressing 'the sincere admiration which I feel for your character and writings' (*OC* XI. 9).

Altogether, the Restoration became a paradigm for Tocqueville. Later, he called it the time of 'great issues' and 'great parties', contrasting it favourably with the July Monarchy and the Second Empire. The fundamental character of the issues debated under the Restoration—the nature and direction of social change in Europe and the prerequisites of representative government—seized and retained Tocqueville's interest. His enthusiasm for the Restoration was, indirectly, a tribute to the sources of his own thought.

21

Tocqueville's good fortune was that he came of age at a time when liberal thought was being transformed in Paris. For the Great Debate of the Restoration was such a turning-point. It transformed not only the agenda but the mode of liberal thought. It created a new genre. Tocqueville's genius lay in his ability to master the issues of the Great Debate and draw out implications lost even on his mentors, Royer-Collard and Guizot.

Why did the Great Debate have such a profound influence on liberal thought? After the fall of Napoleon and return of Louis XVIII in 1815, liberals led by the *Doctrinaires* dominated the early governments of the Restoration, but, in 1820, the assassination of the heir to the throne led to the emergence of an ultra-royalist government ('more royalist than the King', the wags said) which, under Villèle, embarked on an ambitious legislative programme in the mid-1820s. Liberals interpreted that programme as nothing less than an attempt to re-create an aristocratic society and government in France. The result was a prolonged, far-ranging debate between the liberals and ultra-royalists, which dominated the Chamber of Deputies, the press, and pamphleteering for several years.

The Great Debate imposed an agenda on liberal argument. Liberals had to demonstrate that what the ultras proposed was not only unjust but impossible—that even if ultras could temporarily command political power, long-standing social and economic changes in France made their aristocratic programme of hardly more than antiquarian interest. Legislative fiat, even if backed by military force and clerical pressure, could not undo the sub-division of property, market economy and social mobility characteristic of nineteenth-century France. In the eyes of the liberals, the rural gentry and former *émigrés* who composed the ultra-royalist majority were like sleepwalkers dreaming of a manorial and deferential France which no longer existed.

In attacking the ultras' legislative programme, liberals made the 'destruction of aristocracy' in France their theme, a destruction which they traced back many centuries. The 1789 Revolution was thus subject to significant reinterpretation. The Revolution was seen as formalizing changes in French society and adjusting the structure of French government to those changes, rather than being in itself the primary source of social change. Liberals learned to make a careful distinction between social structure and political institutions. They also assumed that the former had causal priority. Guizot made that assumption explicit as early as 1822:

It is by the study of political institutions that most writers . . . have sought to understand the state of a society, the degree or type of its civilization. It would have been wiser to study first the society itself in order to understand its political institutions. Before becoming a cause, political institutions are an effect; a society produces them before being modified by them. Thus, instead of looking to the system or form of government in order to understand the state of the people, it is the state of the people that must be examined first in order to know what must have been, what could have been its government.

Society, its composition, the manner of life of individuals according to their social position, the relation of the different classes, the condition (*l'état*) of persons especially—that is the first question which demands attention from . . . the inquirer who seeks to understand how a people are governed.

In order to understand political institutions, it is necessary to understand the different social conditions (classes) and their relations. In order to understand the different social conditions, it is necessary to understand the nature and relations of properties. (*Essays on the History of France* [1822], 87–90)

The implication was obvious: social structure set limits on political choice. If, for example, the subdivision of property, the spread of education, and social mobility had undermined the caste system inherited from feudalism, then no government—whatever its bravado—could re-create an aristocratic society in France.

Clearly, the liberals' new emphasis on the distinction between social structure and political institutions did not result from mere curiosity. It also reflected polemical needs. When liberals pondered the development of French institutions since the Middle Ages— an exercise which reached its most original form in Guizot's *History of Civilization* (1828–30)—they found reason not only for satisfaction but for disquiet. Changes in society since the heyday of feudalism seemed to them beneficial and just, but the changes in French government were far less reassuring.

Consequently, Restoration liberals found that they had to argue on two fronts—congratulating themselves on what Madame de Staël called the 'progress of equality' and what Guizot called the 'rise of the middle classes', while criticizing the bureaucratic form of the state which had developed since Richelieu and Louis XIV. The changes in society culminating in the triumph of civil equality in 1789 conformed to natural justice, but the growth of centralized power and destruction of local autonomy seemed, to say the least, dangerous.

Napoleon's tyrannical state was still vivid in the liberals' minds, for Restoration France had retained much of the administrative structure of Napoleonic France. The *Doctrinaires*—Royer-Collard, Barante, and Guizot—had served in the Ministry of the Interior at the outset of the Restoration. They knew the French state machine from within. They understood how local government had been reduced to local administration, with even mayors responsible to officials in Paris rather than to local electors. Local initiatives languished. Local opinion could be ignored. In the liberals' eyes, it was only because the ultra-royalists controlled such a powerful state machine that they could delude themselves into supposing that they might reverse the social changes which had long since undermined aristocracy in France.

The need to argue on two fronts—to defend the democratic direction of social change, while criticizing the tyrannical form of the French state—shaped the contours of Restoration liberalism and helps to account for its originality. The *Doctrinaires* were obliged to explore, in quite a new way, the relationship between changes in social structure and changes in the form of government. In doing so, they lost some of the optimism of proto-liberal thought, coming to differ both from seventeenth-century Social Contract Theory and from the eighteenth-century Scottish Enlightenment.

Seventeenth-century Social Contract theorists such as Locke had argued from an ahistorical 'state of nature' and had been concerned chiefly with the question of political right. By contrast, Restoration liberals had first of all to conduct an argument about social fact, about the nature and direction of social change in France since the feudal period. They could not therefore proceed simply by laying down assumptions about human nature, and arguing deductively from those assumptions to conclusions about the 'proper' organization of society and government. They could not dispense with history.

Yet Restoration liberals could not afford merely to analyse the course of social change either. Undoubtedly they drew on sociological ideas which had emerged in the eighteenth century with Montesquieu and the Scottish Enlightenment. What has been called the 'Four Stages' theory developed by Scots such as Adam Smith, Adam Ferguson, and John Millar—in which social development was traced through (a) hunting and gathering, (b) nomadic or pastoral, (c) agricultural, and (d) commercial stages—relied upon the 'mode of subsistence' to identify each stage. Other social practices were then related functionally to it. Thus, the eighteenth-century Scots had become adept at tracing changes in property rights, social stratification, family structure, the role of women, and even religion to changes in the mode of subsistence.

Restoration liberals undoubtedly drew on such ideas when they began to analyse the nature and direction of social change in France, but they joined to sociological analysis a far more urgent concern with the form of government, with constitutional issues. Eighteenth-century Scots had not been confronted by a powerful state machine of the French kind. Nor had they faced anything like the reactionary programme of the ultra-royalists. The Scots, it is true, had anxieties about the effect of the division of labour on citizenship or civic virtue, which they expressed in the older language of classical republicanism. But they did not set a new agenda for political theory or develop a new vocabulary to set such an agenda. Yet that is just what Restoration liberals were obliged to do.

The *Doctrinaires* sought to understand how changes in the form of French government had 'sprung from' social changes and to what extent the powerful state machine inherited from Napoleon was inevitable in a modern democratic society. Was decentralization really possible? Their need to understand the relationship between social and political change led Restoration liberals to put forward a theory of 'irresistible' movement from an 'aristocratic' to a 'democratic' society, which drew attention to a political threat posed by the new structure of society. Social levelling or 'atomization' had resulted in 'centralization', the destruction of local autonomy.

Liberals argued that destruction of the intermediate bodies which previously dispersed and localized power had led to an almost unlimited growth of central power, to the development of a bureaucratic form of the state. In 1822 Royer-Collard used the image of *la société en poussière* (the atomized society)—an image with roots in Edmund Burke's eloquent *Reflections on the Revolution in France* (1790)—to point to the centralization which threatens a democratic society.

We have seen the old society perish, and with it that crowd of domestic institutions and independent magistracies which it carried within it . . ., true republics within the monarchy. These institutions did not, it is true, share sovereignty; but they opposed to it everywhere limits which were defended obstinately. Not one of them has survived. The revolution has left only individuals standing. It has dissolved even the (so to speak) physical association of the commune. This is a spectacle without precedent! Before now one had seen only in philosophers' books a nation so decomposed and reduced to its ultimate constituents.

From an atomized society has emerged centralization. There is no need to look elsewhere for its origin. Centralization has not arrived with its head erect, with the authority of a principle; rather, it has developed modestly, as a consequence, a necessity. Indeed, where there are only individuals, all business which is not theirs is necessarily public business, the business of the state. Where there are no independent magistrates, there are only agents of central power. That is how we have become an *administered* people, under the hand of irresponsible civil servants, themselves centralized in the power of which they are agents. ('On the liberty of the press', *Discours*, 2 January 1822)

Royer-Collard's image drew attention to the way the contractual theory which liberals inherited from the seventeenth-century—with its habit of moving between a 'natural individual' and the association of all, or the state—made no provision for intermediate associations. Indeed, he suggested that tacit distrust of such associations had helped to create the new Leviathan.

Only a few years later, in *Democracy in America*, Tocqueville was to make Royer-Collard's image the most powerful of all sociological images. Evidently he had found that image compelling from his first encounter with it. It was compelling because it ruled out any simple or naïve optimism about the relationship between social and political change—drawing attention to the way the new democratic structure of society could develop at the expense of local autonomy. 'From an atomized society has emerged centralization.'

In the late 1820s, Tocqueville learned to think in the terms put forward by the *Doctrinaires*. By taking on these terms, he also took on certain assumptions. Restoration liberals called the emergent society 'democratic', whereas eighteenth-century Scots had called it 'commercial'. The difference is revealing. The Scottish usage made the 'mode of subsistence' perhaps the crucial factor in social change, whereas French liberals emphasized the different beliefs or norms which helped to constitute aristocratic and democratic societies—the former marked by inequality of rights and conditions, the latter by equality of rights and conditions. In that way, French liberals defined the Social Contract tradition's assumption of 'natural equality' into a type of social structure, and distanced themselves from the ultra-royalists who assumed that an aristocratic society was the only type of society properly so-called.

By using 'democratic' to refer to a type of society the *Doctrinaires* not only dramatized their opposition to the ultra-royalists, they also distanced themselves from the pre-revolutionary cult of antiquity. As Madame de Staël and Benjamin Constant (in his 'On Ancient and Modern Liberty', 1817) had argued, the democracy of the ancient *polis* or city-state was radically incomplete. For the 'citizens' were a privileged caste, while slaves, women, and the foreign-born had no civil status or rights. This suggested that modern democracy could not only stand comparison with ancient democracy, but was, from a moral standpoint, superior to it. It is probably no accident that Constant, Madame de Staël, and Guizot were Protestants. Their suggestion that the gradual penetration of Christian norms underlay the transformation of European society—the movement from aristocracy to democracy—was designed to break the link between Christianity and aristocracy which the ultra-royalists took for granted.

These Protestant liberals saw the distinctive mark of Christianity as its insistence on the basic equality of humans, so that no one had a moral obligation to obey another as such. Hence, they concluded, the right to command and the duty to obey should no longer be written into separate, hereditary social roles as in an aristocratic society. In that respect, liberalism was analogous to Christian morality. The fundamental or root concept of liberalism was also human equality: its commitment to 'equal liberty' sprang

27

from that. Guizot especially emphasized the analogy between Christian morality and liberal assumptions. He made it the central claim of The *Society of Christian Morality* which he helped to found in the mid-1820s, to rally liberals and combat ultra-royalism. Tocqueville apparently joined that society. If so, it was an important step in his 'conversion' to liberalism, and left him with a sense of the importance of Guizot's analogy.

Protestant liberal assumptions suggested that the idea of public authority founded on the consent of the governed was not a mere chimera. For the ultra-royalists, on the other hand, democratic authority was a contradiction in terms, as they defined 'authority' in such a way that it entailed a hierarchical or aristocratic society. Thus, instead of attempting to understand the development of European society, the ultras' argument remained wholly prescriptive. In their eyes, departure from an aristocratic model of society threatened to produce not another type of society, but non-society—anarchy or the reign of brute force. By introducing the idea of democratic authority, Restoration liberals rejected the ultras' strategy of argument. But that made it all the more important for them to scrutinize the growth of state power, which had accompanied the emergence of a democratic society in France.

Royer-Collard's image of an atomized society leading to centralization was designed to do just that. It drew attention to the way a democratic society, by freeing individuals from traditional ties of status and dependence, destroyed the corporate character of society. Intermediate bodies, which had once served to disperse power and authority, were the casualties. For only individuals now stood, where once there had been privileged orders, provincial estates, guilds, *parlements*, and manorial courts. The beneficiary was the state, which alone could claim to represent the interests of all equally. For the state created and protected the structure of individual rights which helped to constitute a democratic society and thus the growth of the state was *necessarily* or intrinsically connected with the progress of social equality.

But what form of the state? Was a bureaucratic form of the state now unavoidable? By 1828–9, Tocqueville had come to rely on the *Doctrinaires'* categories to understand social change and its political consequences. However, the image of an 'atomized' society leading to 'centralization' began to raise questions in his mind—

questions which eventually led him to reject the English model of government as a 'solution' for France (the solution recommended by older liberals such as Madame de Staël) and turn his attention instead to American federalism.

If we are to understand how the categories of Restoration liberalism both shaped the young Tocqueville's thinking and led him, in turn, to question and revise those categories, we must look more closely at the Great Debate of the 1820s—first at the argument about social and economic change, and then at the argument about political change.

To combat the ultra-royalist programme after 1820, liberals began to argue that since the eleventh century in Europe one type of society had given way irreversibly to another, 'aristocracy' to 'democracy'. But what did that involve? It involved, crucially, the destruction of a caste society. Feudalism had originally created two castes: the ownership of land by a military aristocracy, the nobles, had carried with it the right to govern those permanently attached to the land, the serfs. Political rights had then been simply one facet of property rights. Liberals argued that the erosion of feudalism began with the rebirth of towns and commerce in the later Middle Ages, the growth of a market economy leading to the multiplication of wants and to a more elaborate division of labour. But not only that. It led to the emergence of a new, intermediate social class, the middle class or bourgeoisie. The distinctive thing about this new class was that its members were free to move about, buy and sell.

In France, the fifteenth to the eighteenth century witnessed the gradual collapse of the original castes of feudal society into this new or 'middling' social condition. In order to compete with the consumption of the new commercial class, the old nobility began to sell its lands to raise money, while there was a steady movement of people into the towns to escape from feudal oppression. The middle class or bourgeoisie grew in numbers and in wealth, and embodied new norms of 'natural' equality. Its growth coincided with the emergence of a structure of individual rights, not least property rights.

Thus, European history became a story about the movement from inequality of rights and conditions towards equality of rights

29

and conditions. By the eighteenth century, despite the formal inequalities surviving from a caste society, the dynamism and wealth of the middle classes had brought about a crucial shift in the balance of social power. In wealth, education and way of life, there was little difference between the urban middle classes and the *noblesse* in France, while in the countryside most of the peasants had not only ceased to be serfs but had become landowners. A new 'democratic' type of society had come into being. By 1789 it was only waiting, so to speak, for the sanction of formal equality of rights.

Ironically, the ultra-royalist programme itself played an important role in enabling liberals to deepen their understanding of the irreversible transformation of French society. For the ultra proposals to restore aristocratic privilege drew attention to one institution after another which had undergone radical change since the feudal period. Liberal criticisms of ultra proposals therefore helped to make clear the ways in which a democratic society differed from an aristocratic society. They revealed the primary elements of social structure—property rights, stratification, the type of family, religious belief, the conditions of work, social and geographical mobility. These elements or points of comparison made it possible to assess the extent of social change in France since the eleventh century with increasing precision and subtlety.

Tocqueville was a beneficiary of Restoration liberals' refinement of sociological argument. It is no accident that soon after arriving in the United States, in 1831, he wrote back to France asking that a copy of Guizot's *History of Civilization*—a sophisticated digest of liberal arguments in the Great Debate—be sent to him in America, since he wanted to use Guizot's analysis to identify the crucial elements of a democratic social structure. In fact, he had already made use of Guizot's analysis. In the late 1820s, Guizot's *History* had helped to persuade him of the futility of the ultra-royalist attempt to restore aristocratic privilege in France.

The ambition of the ultra-royalists' programme in the 1820s was breathtaking. That was what, finally, made it so instructive. Ultra proposals threatened to destroy the distinction between Church and State by giving the clergy once again an important role in government; to make sacrilege a crime punishable by death; to restore primogeniture and entail in order to prevent landed estates slipping away from the old *noblesse*; to restrict the (already limited) suffrage in such a way that the political class was limited to major landowners; to overthrow the 'career open to talents' proclaimed by the Revolution in favour of privileged positions for the sons of the *noblesse*; to restore censorship of books and limit freedom of the press; to close University lectures; to abolish trial by jury; to modify the conditions of work by restricting the role of contract; and to restore the father's authority over other members of the family. There were even rumours that the ultras intended to reintroduce the guild system and so put an end to the free market in labour. Altogether, the ultras seemed bent not just on ignoring the Constitutional Charter granted by Louis XVIII in 1814, but on undermining the whole structure of nineteenth-century French society.

These ultra-royalist proposals forced the liberal opposition to explore systematically the differences between the 'old' society and the 'new', between 'aristocracy' and 'democracy'. Liberals laid ever increasing emphasis on the way ultra proposals were not only unjust but were misconceived—running against a powerful causal nexus which legislative fiat could not overcome. Liberals argued that, in contrast to the subsistence agriculture of early feudalism, the free circulation of property had created such great economic prosperity and social interdependence that the reintroduction of primogeniture and entail in the hope of recreating a rural aristo-cracy in France would be bound to fail. The advanced division of labour, social and geographical mobility, and higher levels of education in France simply could not now be undone. These were foundational facts which any legislator had to take into account, even if he wished to modify them. By the same token, the ultras' challenge to the principle of equal access to careers and promotion by merit—for example, by restricting the officer class to aristo-crats—would come up against democratic expectations so deeply engrained as to be insurmountable.

In the eyes of the liberals, the ultras' attempt to restore an earlier role for the Church was just as foolhardy. The Villèle ministry and Charles X (who had succeeded Louis XVIII in 1824) lent their support to efforts by Catholic orders to 'rechristianize' the country, efforts which led to processions of expiation and penance through-out the cities and towns of France. The coronation of Charles X in

31

Reims, in 1825, seemed to the liberal public a complete medieval throwback, with the king prostrating himself before the archbishop of Paris. There were suggestions that the Villèle ministry might try to introduce other 'medieval' measures—in particular, that it might abolish freedom of religion and return control of education to the clergy.

In reply, liberals conceded that the Church had played a far greater role when the priesthood were the only educated people in society. But the growth of cities and spread of secular learning had long since changed that. These social facts could not suddenly be abrogated. Besides, the desire of the ultras to use the Church as an instrument of social control, to reinstall a deference to the old privileged classes which had long since disappeared in France, ran counter to the very Christian beliefs which the ultras claimed to defend. Thus, Royer-Collard intoned in the Chamber against ultra-royalist restrictions on freedom of thought and publication, as well as the banning of university lectures: 'In the eyes of this law, it was a great imprudence on the part of God to leave man, on the day of creation, free and intelligent in the midst of the universe.'

For Tocqueville, who was pursuing legal studies in Paris, the ultra-royalist assault on a society founded on the principle of civil equality was not only fascinating but terrifying. Images of civil war had plagued his childhood. But his adult sense of the danger of opposing social change can be traced to these years. His letters in the late 1820s betray not only Tocqueville's contempt for the blindness of his own class but his belief that it was unjust to seek to restore privilege. Writing to Beaumont, in 1828, and describing the rise of the bourgeoisie at the expense of the feudal aristocracy and the serfs, he commented:

It gained everything which the two other orders lost, for it approached more than they did the natural condition of the human race. . . . After all, a reasonable equality is the only condition natural to man, since the [European] peoples have approached it from such different starting points and moving along such different paths. (*OC* VIIIa. 56–7)

Clearly, Tocqueville's understanding of the direction of social change and his acceptance of the liberal principle of 'equal liberty' were already firmly established. He had also come to detest the often cynical alliance between the ultra-royalists and the Catholic

hierarchy in France—attempts to use the Church as an instrument
of political control.

Just a few years later Tocqueville described to an English friend
the misconceived religious policy of the Restoration Monarchy.
'The Bourbons returned with the idea that they had to support the
throne with the altar . . .'

The clergy become political authorities through the weight given to their
recommendations. Places were often given on the basis of the belief of
those who competed for them rather than on the basis of capacity. At least
so it was believed. As the Restoration became more settled, the union of
Church and State become more and more obvious. A law was promulgated
to punish with the utmost rigour the profanation of religious vessels and
theft in churches. All the archbishops and many bishops entered the
Chamber of Peers. The nation was, or rather believed itself to be, governed
by priests and saw their influence everywhere. Then what is called the
Voltairean spirit was reborn, that is to say, the attitude of systematic
hostility and mockery not only of the ministers of religion but of religion
itself, Christianity in all its forms . . . Caricatures, theatres and songs were
dominated by bitter satires against the clergy and took on an inconceivable
violence. I was then carrying out functions analogous to those of a royal
procurator, and I noticed that every time a priest had the misfortune of
being accused of a crime or infraction, juries, in general so indulgent,
nearly always condemned unanimously. (*OC* [Beaumont] II. 44–66)

Politically the result was inevitable. 'Nearly all liberals, that is the
great majority of the nation, became irreligious out of political
principle' (ibid.). Because the clergy had embraced the cause of
arbitrary royal power and social privilege, liberals concluded that
impiety was a necessary form of opposition.

The influence of particular debates in the mid-1820s on the
young Tocqueville is not merely a matter of conjecture. In 1826–7,
while visiting Italy with his brother Edouard, he composed a
journal in which reverberations of the Great Debate can be heard.
This was just after discussions in the Chambers and in the press
about the ultra bill (February 1826) to reintroduce primogeniture
and entail, and suppress the Civil Code's stipulation that property
be shared equally among children—a stipulation which ultras saw
as the single greatest obstacle to the rebirth of aristocracy in
France. In observing the pattern of Sicilian landholding, Tocqueville goes out of his way to emphasize the importance of subdivid-

ing land among the peasants in order to increase productivity. He employs an argument used by liberal spokesmen to show that the aggregation of land in England did not prove the beneficial effects of primogeniture and entail. Rather, it was a later stage in the development of a market economy, when land becomes a repository for acquired wealth rather than a hindrance to its multiplication. The importance which Tocqueville learned to attach to the law of 'equal shares' emerged when he wrote *Democracy in America*. It became, in his eyes, the engine of social levelling which he found almost complete in the United States. In fact, Tocqueville exaggerated its importance on the American scene, but even his misjudgement is evidence of the extent to which he used issues from the Great Debate to understand American institutions.

If a list were made of the issues debated in Paris in the mid-1820s, and that list were placed alongside the table of contents of *Democracy in America* (1835), it would reveal a remarkable overlap. Tocqueville turned many of those debates into chapters of his book. They provided him with a guide to the most prominent features of a democratic society, enabling him to lay bare its structure in a way that astonished even his American readers. The progress of social equality, the subdivision of property, the separation of Church and State, religious freedom and its consequences, the importance of voluntary associations, freedom of the press and trial by jury, the role of social and geographical mobility—these themes from *Democracy in America* reflect questions first raised in Tocqueville's mind by the Great Debate. That is the sense in which he sought American answers to French questions, something he freely admitted later to his friend Louis de Kergolay.

But why *American* answers? Why did Tocqueville come to think that American institutions might have an important didactic potential? Here, too, the Great Debate provides a crucial clue, for in addition to the analysis of economic and social change conducted by the liberals, the Great Debate had a political dimension—and that dimension was no less formative for Tocqueville

At the outset of the Restoration, liberals such as Madame de Staël retained a kind of pre-Revolutionary optimism, assuming that the destruction of social privilege would lead to the triumph of parliamentary government on the English model with *de facto* local autonomy. By the 1820s, however, liberals such as Royer-Collard and Barante were less sure. They had worked in the Ministry of the Interior before 1820. They had seen the extent to which power was concentrated at the centre in France, in a bureaucratic machine which had destroyed local autonomy.

By 1822–3, as we have seen, Royer-Collard was arguing that the destruction of intermediate institutions, such as *parlements* and provincial estates, had left only individuals standing—formally equal perhaps, but equally weak. Almost nothing remained to curb the growth of central power. In a democratic society, Royer-Collard concluded gloomily, liberty of the press, freedom of association, and trial by jury were the only barriers to an excessive concentration of power at the centre.

Was a bureaucratic state, a potentially tyrannical form of the state, the unavoidable consequence of a democratic society, its structural weakness? If so, local autonomy was a thing of the past. The younger *Doctrinaires*, Barante and Guizot, refused to be so pessimistic, however. They began to ask new questions about why, by the late seventeenth century, England had developed representative government with local autonomy, while France had succumbed to royal despotism and centralization. In order to understand why, they began to compare the development of French and English institutions since the early Middle Ages—just the comparison which the young Tocqueville decided to make in the mid-1820s. He was almost certainly following their lead.

Class conflict in France became the *Doctrinaires'* theme. It was a theme which the bitter struggles between the ultra-royalists and the liberal bourgeoisie in the 1820s could hardly fail to suggest. Barante and Guizot traced the difference between French and English development back to the early Middle Ages. They argued that the Norman Conquest had created a stronger monarchy in England, a more centralized form of feudalism necessary to keep a hostile population under control. By the thirteenth century the growth of royal power led the English nobility to band together to limit royal pretensions, and to strengthen their hand, the aristocracy called leaders of the Commons to Parliament. The resulting *de facto* alliance aimed at limiting royal power had crucial effects in turn on the structure of English society and government. It meant that the monarchy had to share sovereign power with parliament, while the effect on social structure was no less dramatic—a gradual merger of the original feudal class with the leaders of the Commons, creating a 'natural aristocracy' founded on wealth and education rather than merely on birth. By 1828 Tocqueville understood this: 'Once Parliament had been created, the Lords nearly always sought out the Commons and supported them on all occasions, which served slowly to unite the two orders which were such irreconcilable enemies elsewhere in Europe' (*OC* VIIIa. 60).

The French story was strikingly different. In the early Middle Ages the French monarchy had been reduced to little more than a symbol, while real power was dispersed among the feudal nobility. The consequence was that when the towns revived and needed an ally to struggle against their local feudal oppressors, they turned, *faute de mieux*, to the Crown. Thus, there grew up an alliance between the Crown and the bourgeoisie aimed at the destruction of the nobility's local power, an alliance which in the long run had dramatic consequences for the structure of French society and government. Bitter rivalry between the nobility and bourgeoisie prevented the development of a 'natural aristocracy', while the struggle against the nobility's local power led to the centralization of power in the Crown, in a bureaucratic form of the state. The *Doctrinaires* thus presented the destruction of local autonomy in France as an unintended consequence of the destruction of aristocracy.

That was the argument of Prosper de Barante's short book *On Aristocracy and the Communes*, published in 1822. Barante argued that, by relying on the Crown and steadily transferring political authority to it, the French bourgeoisie had created a kind of monster, for the Napoleonic state was only a more systematic form of the despotic state which had been created long before by Richelieu and Louis XIV. Did Tocqueville read Barante's book? We cannot be sure, but circumstantial evidence makes it highly likely. Barante urged decentralization on the French. He argued that restoring local autonomy and initiative was a necessary condition for recreating a political élite or natural aristocracy in France. Local autonomy also offered the best hope of overcoming class conflict, by encouraging classes to co-operate at the local level.

That was the only alternative to bureaucratic tyranny in a democratic society.

There was an unresolved problem, however. For how could local autonomy be combined with the hierarchy of legal authority embodied in the idea of state 'sovereignty' which was required for uniform laws throughout the nation? It seemed that the state might dissolve if local autonomy were to become a reality. Under the Restoration, that spectre had emerged whenever *la charte provinciale* (the Provincial Charter)—extending representative institutions from the national to local and regional levels—had become an issue. In response, Madame de Staël, Benjamin Constant, and Guizot had all suggested that 'a new federalism' might be the next stage in the development of representative government. In the 1828–30 lectures which Tocqueville attended, Guizot drew attention to the intellectual and moral preconditions of federalism—contrasting it with the dispersal of power in feudal society, where force rather than right had been the guarantee of decentralization. Feudal society did not yet have the moral and intellectual development, Guizot argued, required for a political system, such as federalism, which formally dispersed authority.

What the *Doctrinaires* did, then, was to redefine the major political problem facing modern democratic societies. No longer concerned with the basis of political obligation or the limits of legitimate state action in the fashion of seventeenth-century political philosophers, they made another question central. Could a balance between central power and local autonomy be found in a democratic society—that is, a society in which local autonomy is no longer protected by aristocratic power? At issue was nothing less than the idea of the state itself. For, as Royer-Collard argued, even the separation of powers in central government recommended by Montesquieu (who drew on England as a model) did not provide any effective guarantee against the destruction of local autonomy, legitimated by an appeal to the state's sovereignty. That, it is clear in retrospect, was the beginning of the rejection of the English 'solution' which had previously dominated liberal prescriptions for 'ending' the French Revolution.

By 1828 Tocqueville accepted the *Doctrinaires'* formulation of the great political problem facing modern democratic societies. In that year he wrote excitedly to Beaumont:

There are two great disadvantages to be avoided in the organization of a people: either all social power is united at one point or it is dispersed among the regions. Each of these has its advantages and disadvantages. When everything is joined in a single bundle, once the bundle is broken, everything falls apart and the people disappear. When power is disseminated, action is evidently circumscribed, but resistance is everywhere. I don't know if a balance between these two extremes can be found. (*OC* VIIIa. 53)

Neither the liberals nor the ultras had so far put forward a persuasive answer to the question of how to find a balance between central power and local autonomy. The liberal prescription of adopting English parliamentary institutions overlooked the fact that in England local autonomy was guaranteed not by parliamentary sovereignty, but by the existence of a powerful 'natural aristocracy'—something which did not exist in France. The ultras' prescription was even less convincing, for, denying the social and economic changes which had transformed France over a number of centuries, they were trying to reconstruct society on the old basis of privilege, to recreate local autonomy by way of aristocracy.

Evidently these unsatisfactory solutions to the problem of finding a balance between central power and local autonomy led Tocqueville to speculate whether American federalism might provide a better model for reform than English parliamentary government. We do not know exactly when, though there is an intriguing letter he wrote in the 1820s criticizing his cousin, the writer Chateaubriand, for confusing the new independence of South American states from Spain with 'real' self-government (on the North American model?). In 1828 Tocqueville met the American historian and biographer of Washington, Jared Sparks, in Paris. Sparks would have reminded him of his hero Malesherbes' enthusiasm for the new republic and its experiment with self-government. Malesherbes had befriended the American delegates to Paris in the 1780s, Benjamin Franklin and Thomas Jefferson, and also saw to it that the first official French representative to the Continental Congress was a cousin, the Chevalier de la Luzerne. Apparently Malesherbes had looked upon the United States as a place of exile if he were driven from France by the Revolution. Certainly, he encouraged Chateaubriand to visit the new nation— a journey which enabled Chateaubriand to publish *Réné* and *Atala* on his return and led to literary fame. It is unlikely that these associations were lost on the precocious young Tocqueville.

It has been argued that Tocqueville became interested in the question of centralization only in the mid-1830s—something which would make his journey to the United States far more accidental. But that is clearly wrong. By 1828, as we have seen, Tocqueville accepted the *Doctrinaires'* definition of the urgent political problem facing modern democratic societies. He was also familiar with his father's work for the parliamentary committee examining ways of extending the representative principle to local government (*la charte provinciale*) in 1828–9. In his memoir of Tocqueville's life, Beaumont suggests that Tocqueville had for some years pondered the questions which led him to visit America, while a letter which his friend Chabrol wrote to Tocqueville in America teases him about his long-standing concern with the issue of centralization. But the decisive confirmation comes from Tocqueville himself. 'It is nearly ten years that I have believed some of the things which I described to you just now. I only went to America to clarify them', he wrote in 1835 (*OC* XIII. 1. 374). What has misled commentators is the fact that Tocqueville wrote to his father, from America, asking for exact details of the French administrative system and stressing his own ignorance. But that was another matter. Until then, he had been concerned only with the general or theoretical aspects of the debate.

It is not possible to follow the steps by which Tocqueville came to reject the English 'solution' or when he first began to conjecture that American institutions might be a more profitable model for reform of the over-centralized French state. But that this was the background which informed his journey to America and informed his observations there can hardly be doubted. Just a few weeks after reaching New York, and long before he began to examine American political institutions—while Beaumont and he were fully occupied with the 'penitentiary business' which was the pretext for their journey—Tocqueville wrote to his cousin Louis de Kergolay:

We are heading for a democracy without limits, . . . pushed by an irresistible force. All efforts to arrest this process will only result in temporary halts . . . I am obliged to think that the Bourbons, instead of trying to reinforce an aristocratic principle which is dying among us, ought to have worked with all their strength to give new motives of order and stability to democracy. In my opinion, the communal and departmental system ought from the outset to have attracted all their attention. Instead of living from day to day with the communal institutions left by Bonaparte, they ought to have hastened to modify them, initiate people gradually into the management of their own affairs, . . . creating local interests and founding if at all possible those *habits and legal ideas* which are in my opinion the only possible counterweight to democracy. (*OC* XIIIa. 233)

The governing ideas of *Democracy in America* are already present—the 'irresistible' democratic revolution and the need to find a means of preserving local autonomy in the face of centralizing pressures.

Clearly, the Great Debate of the 1820s provided the conceptions which led Tocqueville to America and governed his observations there. The Great Debate provided him with what amounted to an hypothesis. If French centralization was an unintended consequence of the struggle against aristocratic privilege, then the United States—which had never known feudalism or aristocratic privilege—should make it possible to demonstrate that a democratic society need not succumb to centralization. American institutions might reveal that French centralization was only a transitional problem.

3 *Democracy in America* (1835)

By writing *Democracy in America* (1835) Tocqueville attempted something extraordinary—the overturn of the established European idea of the state. It was an idea to which Jean Bodin's *Republic* (1576) and Thomas Hobbes's *Leviathan* (1651) had made perhaps the most important contribution. Bodin and Hobbes had put forward the concept of 'sovereignty' in order to identify unlimited and indivisible authority over men and things within a given territory as the hallmark of the state, its defining attribute. According to their account, positive or state-made law was simply the 'command' of a sovereign agency.

Tocqueville was now convinced that such an idea of the state had outlived its usefulness. It did not suit the new democratic society being consolidated in Europe. 'A new political science is needed for a world itself quite new', he insisted at the outset of *Democracy in America* (1835). In his view the equalizing of social conditions made a new idea of the state indispensible, for the established idea was a product of class conflicts during the transition from aristocracy to democracy. That emerged in its stipulation that within a state some 'sovereign' agency must have a *monopoly* of authority. Doubtless such a stipulation had been useful in attacking feudal jurisdictions. But now it lent itself to tyranny for it could be used to justify an extreme centralization of power. Unfortunately, the prolonged struggle to destroy feudal jurisdiction had blinded Europeans to the dangers attending such a stipulation.

The nature of Tocqueville's theoretical enterprise has seldom been appreciated. Indeed, histories of political thought continue to be written without even mentioning him. Ironically, Tocqueville became the victim of his own success. In *Democracy in America* (1835) he sought to reach the widest possible audience, and in order to do so he presented the major steps of his argument through illustrations rather than simply relying on formal definitions and deductive argument. He enabled French readers to see a form of the state they had never before encountered or imagined, a truly decentralized form of the state.

Democracy in America (1835)

The vividness of *Democracy in America* (1835) helped to make it one of the most widely read works of political thought ever published. But this quality has also drawn attention away from the theoretical context of Tocqueville's argument. His friend Beaumont tells the story of Tocqueville meeting an Englishman who had read *Democracy in America* and who congratulated Tocqueville especially for his success in avoiding general ideas! Yet, as we have seen, Tocqueville was pursuing a theoretical question which had been raised under the Restoration, but had not been answered. The question was whether a decentralized form of the state was possible in a democratic society—a society which, *ex hypothesi*, lacked a governing class. Appeals to the English model of government for guidance no longer seemed helpful. Montesquieu had relied on the English model to argue that power could be dispersed only by preserving an aristocratic society. However, if the guarantees provided by an aristocratic social structure were removed, local autonomy in England looked precarious. For parliamentary sovereignty provided no intrinsic obstacle to extreme centralization, once the traditional local hegemony of the upper and middle classes was challenged.

It seemed unlikely that a society which lacked a governing class, even on the open model of the English aristocracy, could govern itself. Was it not bound to fall victim to anarchy or to a new kind of tyranny, a bureaucratic form of the state? The French state machine elaborated by Richelieu and Louis XIV and 'perfected' by Napoleon offered an ominous example. It was that state machine which had proved so resistant to reform under the Restoration, and threatened to make a mockery of representative government.

But the problem was not only practical: a decentralized form of the state also presented theoretical difficulties. Madame de Staël, drawing on the pre-Revolutionary federalist movement, had suggested that federalism represented the next stage of representative government and Benjamin Constant had gone further. In his *Principles of Politics* (1815) he envisaged what he called the 'new federalism', a system in which communes and provinces would control the affairs which concerned them alone, leaving to central government only matters of general concern. Yet in Constant's book the constitutional *means* of securing that goal remained elusive. How, for example, if towns and provinces were given real autonomy could they be made to conform to the general laws of the land? If local officers were elected, and answerable only to local people, what would prevent them embarking on courses which might lead to the dissolution of the state?

In the 1820s Guizot had grappled with the idea of a decentralized state by criticizing the concept of sovereignty which, since Bodin and Hobbes, had been identified as the chief attribute of the state. Guizot argued, though not always clearly, that the concept of sovereignty, understood as some agency or group within the State enjoying a *monopoly* of legal authority, was necessary neither to the idea of the state nor to its practical embodiment. Guizot rejected the claims of any body, whether the Crown, a legislative assembly or even the people at large, to a *monopoly* of right. But about the constitutional means by which legal right could be dispersed within a political system or state to protect local autonomy, he provided no adequate guide, calling only for the separation of powers, bicameralism, the jury system, and freedom of the press.

This is the background for understanding Tocqueville's earliest remarks in letters from America. What struck him immediately was the 'absence of government', by which he meant the absence of the centralized form of the state known in France. A society which *'goes along by itself'* elated him. The vigour of civil society in America seemed to make central government less important. It was the first sign that the hypothesis which had led him to America might be correct. Decentralization *was* possible in a democratic society. Unhampered by class consciousness, the American colonists had proceeded to establish government in what could be called the 'natural' fashion for a democratic society—that is, they first formed themselves into local units of self-government, the township; then proceeded to join together in a regional form of government, the state; and only much later began to envisage and form an association of the states, or national government.

In coming to understand that progression as 'natural', Tocqueville had made the discovery that the lack of class consciousness in America was crucial. The Great Debate had prepared him for a society in which civil equality gave the middle classes a predominant role. That was already the case in France. But he was not prepared for a society in which status differences deriving from an aristocratic society had disappeared. Despite equality before the law, classes in France continued to differ from one another sharply in attitudes and manners, in their sense of identity. But in the United States people did not feel essentially different from one another. There were, of course, rich and poor, but such differences were regarded as accidental. The feelings of superiority and humiliation did not play a significant role in America. In that respect, American society represented a complete development of the democratic principle. Everyone—with the appalling exception of the black slaves and the indigenous Indians—was, more or less, 'middle class'.

These conclusions about the direction of social change, as well as the political agenda it raised, dominated Tocqueville's introduction to *Democracy in America* (1835). What he saw in the United States convinced him that a decentralized future for democratic societies was possible, but it was possible only if stringent moral and political conditions were met. He wrote in order to identify those conditions for the French.

The book opens with an eloquent account of the progress of social equality in Europe. Tocqueville writes like an aristocrat who has had the vision of a contrary truth, his detached, solemn tones announcing the destruction of one type of society and the advent of another. 'Aristocracy' is giving way to 'democracy' everywhere in the Christian West. 'A great democratic revolution is going on among us.'

If, beginning with the eleventh century, we examine what has happened in France from one half century to another, we shall not fail to perceive that at the end of each of these periods a two-fold revolution has taken place in the state of society. The noble has gone down the social ladder, and the commoner has gone up . . . Every century brings them nearer to each other, and they will soon meet. (*OC* Ia. 4)

Inequality of rights and conditions, which had been extreme under feudalism, was giving way 'throughout the Christian world' to equality of rights and conditions.

Tocqueville brought together everything he had learned from the Great Debate to identify the cumulative social changes which he calls the 'democratic social revolution'. That term itself is revealing—it reveals how he had learned from Restoration Liberals to distinguish social structure from political institutions and to preface any discussion of political institutions with an account of social change. Thus, 'democratic', as Tocqueville used it, refers first of all to a type of society, while 'revolution' refers to gradual changes in social structure rather than to dramatic political events. The 'democratic revolution' refers not to the overthrow of a dynasty but to the emergence of a historically unprecedented type of society, a society founded on the principle of civil equality.

In demonstrating how aristocracy had given way to democracy, Tocqueville relied heavily on issues explored during the 1820s in France, drawing attention to the subdivision of land and new importance of moveable property, to the development of a market economy and the multiplication of wants, to the spread of knowledge and social mobility. The upshot of these changes was that a 'middling' social condition, which had once been exceptional, was rapidly becoming the norm throughout the West. The social extremes represented by the old nobility and uninstructed peasantry were disappearing.

Tocqueville did not however present this revolution in social structure as mere brute fact—as an unintended but overwhelming causal nexus. He presented it as a 'providential' fact. 'The whole book has been written under the influence of a kind of religious awe produced in the author's mind by the view of that irresistible revolution which has advanced for centuries in spite of every obstacle.' Restoration liberals had helped him to see Western history in that way.

If the men of our time should be convinced by attentive observation and sincere reflection that the gradual and progressive development of social equality is at once the past and the future of their history, this discovery alone would confer upon that change the sacred character of a divine decree. To attempt to check democracy would be in that case to resist the will of God.   [*OC* Ia. 5]

Tocqueville's language of 'irresistibility' and 'religious awe' raises a problem, since it might suggest that he believed history to be governed by higher laws which completely override human agency. However, such a conclusion would be mistaken. In order to see why, it is necessary to consider his audience. For Tocqueville was desperately anxious to influence the educated French public of his day—a public divided, as he saw it, between aristocratic and democratic principles.

That conflict appalled him as it meant that France had lost the advantages of an aristocratic society without gaining those of a democratic society. France was stalled in the transition from one type of society to another. 'We have then abandoned whatever advantages the old state of things offered, without receiving any compensation from our present condition', Tocqueville lamented. 'We have destroyed an aristocratic society and we seem inclined to settle down complacently amidst its ruins' (*OC* Ia. 8–9). Class hatreds in France were symptomatic of the continuing conflict between aristocratic and democratic principles.

Tocqueville devoted the *Introduction* to *Democracy in America* (1835) to exploring the problems of the transition. Indeed, that strictly is what he called the 'democratic revolution'. Conflicts of principle, emerging as class conflicts, defined that revolutionary or transitional period. It is here that he moved beyond Restoration liberals. The idea of a transitional period enabled him to argue that the 'atomization' of society and 'centralization' of government were not necessary or permanent features of a democratic society—as Royer-Collard had implied. Rather, they were results of class conflicts during the transition from aristocracy to democracy.

In France, the struggle to destroy aristocratic privilege had by the nineteenth century left classes estranged, the authority of law precarious, and central power enormously increased. The French democratic classes had not become aware, until it was almost too late, that in destroying aristocratic power they had also destroyed local autonomy. Their political ideas, shaped by the struggles of the transition, were inadequate to deal with the threat posed by state power in a levelled or democratic society.

We have destroyed those powers which were able single-handedly to cope with tyranny, but it is central government alone which has inherited all the prerogatives snatched from families, corporations and individuals; so that the sometimes oppressive but often conservative strength of a small number has given way to the weakness of all.

The break-up of fortunes has diminished the distance between rich and poor, but while bringing them closer, it seems to have provided them with new reasons for hating each other, so that with mutual fear and envy they rebuff each other's claim to power. Neither has any conception of rights, and for both force is the only argument in the present and sole guarantee for the future.   (*OC* Ia. 8)

Tocqueville refused to accept that the condition of France in his day represented the final outcome of the democratic social revolution. 'I cannot believe it—God is preparing a more stable and calmer future for European societies.'   (*OC* Ia. 11)
    Such a future would only be possible when democratic principles were uncontested and laws and *mœurs* could develop 'under the sway of democracy'.

One can imagine a society in which all men, regarding the law as their common work, would love it and submit to it without difficulty. Each man having some rights and being sure of the enjoyment of those rights, there would be established between all classes a sort of reciprocal courtesy, as far removed from pride as servility. Understanding its own interests the people would appreciate that in order to enjoy the benefits of society one must shoulder its obligations. Free association of the citizens could then take the place of the individual authority of the nobles, and the state would be protected both from tyranny and from licence.   (*OC* Ia. 7)

That description suggests the role in which Tocqueville would cast American political institutions—they were post-transitional. They were institutions *undistorted* by the conflict between aristocratic and democratic principles since American society had been democratic from the outset. It had never really known feudalism or aristocratic privilege. Consequently, American institutions had not been distorted by prolonged struggles to destroy aristocracy. American political institutions had a didactic potential because 'that country is reaping the benefits of the democratic revolution taking place among us, without having the revolution itself'.   (*OC* Ia. 11)
    The United States made it possible for Tocqueville to argue that a democratic society is compatible with two utterly different political outcomes, with forms of the state as different as American federalism and the over-centralized French state. By itself the democratic social revolution does not guarantee that self-government or free institutions will prevail. On the contrary, the social conflicts which mark that revolutionary or transitional period create serious obstacles to the establishment of free institutions—

attitudes and habits born of class conflict which survive their origins and make it difficult for classes to co-operate in the way that free institutions require. They still prefer to be governed by a remote bureaucratic power than to share local power with their former class enemies.

Alas, such was the case in France. The democratic party had to be weaned away from the Jacobin tradition, which portrayed the centralized state as the only means of social progress. The aristocratic party had to be persuaded that a bureaucratic form of the state was not the only remaining means of social control, the only barrier to anarchy in a society which had been levelled. These attitudes had prevented the French from considering what kind of political system or state is appropriate for a democratic society, a society no longer beset by formal inequalities of status. That is what gave American institutions their instructive potential. They emerged out of a society which had never known social privilege or class conflict of the French sort.

However, before any new 'political science' inspired by American institutions could be applied in France, a fundamental moral choice had to be made, and it was that choice which Tocqueville identified by describing the democratic social revolution as 'irresistible' or 'providential', by investing it with quasi-religious imagery. In his view, that moral choice was a necessary condition of moving beyond the class conflicts which had plagued the transition from aristocracy to democracy in France and taking up the option of free institutions. Unless the correct moral decision was taken, the democratic social revolution might simply result in tyranny.

The Christian nations of our day present an alarming spectacle; the movement which carries them along is already too strong to be halted, but it is not yet so swift that we must despair of directing it. Our fate is in our hands, but soon it may pass beyond control. (*OC* Ia. 5)

What, then, was the decision Tocqueville had in mind? It was the decision to acknowledge that the democratic revolution was irresistible because it was just—that is, because it was morally irresistible. It was the decision Tocqueville himself had made in the 1820s.

Tocqueville was struck by a contradiction within the views of each French party, a contradiction between its moral principles and its political programme. 'It is as if the natural bond that joins the opinions of man to his tastes, and his actions to his principles, was now broken', he observed. 'The harmony that has always been observed between the feelings and the ideas of mankind appears to be dissolved and all the laws of moral analogy to be abolished' (*OC* Ia. 9). The contradiction within the views of each party gave him hope, however, for it suggested that each party had been carried beyond its real opinions in the course of the conflict. It suggested that the two parties in France shared intuitions of justice.

The class struggles of the transition had resulted in a dangerous moral confusion in France. The aristocratic party refused to acknowledge the egalitarianism implicit in Christian belief, while the democratic party attacked the Church because it had been part of an aristocratic society. Tocqueville's response was to draw attention to the analogy between Christian morality and civil equality—first suggested by Guizot and The Society of Christian Morality—in order to weaken the anti-democratic ardour of the aristocratic party and the anti-religious ardour of the democratic party. 'Christianity, which has declared all men equal in the sight of God, cannot hesitate to acknowledge all citizens equal before the law.' The analogy was designed to reveal a potentially shared conception of justice, a conception founded on the assumption of moral or natural equality.

If the two parties in France could be brought to recognize the analogy between Christian morality and civil equality, the most important step towards restoring a consensus in France would have been taken. For, in Tocqueville's view, it was axiomatic that the ultimate source of social stability was shared belief. 'One cannot establish the reign of liberty without that of *mœurs*, and *mœurs* cannot be firmly founded without beliefs.'

Tocqueville's use of the analogy and of religious imagery did not merely suggest that the democratic revolution was irresistible because it was just, however. It also raised the possibility that Christian beliefs had, over the centuries, made a crucial contribution to that sense of justice and thereby to the democratic revolution. For Tocqueville repeatedly asserted that it was the 'Christian nations' which were undergoing this great social transformation.

49

Yet he did not quite commit himself to the proposition that Christian beliefs had constrained the direction of social change in the West. His own doubts probably prevented that. He did not wish to oversimplify the historical causes. But there was also another reason. He wanted to weaken the association of democracy with disbelief, without rekindling the anti-clericalism of the French left and without being dismissed as a Catholic apologist. He was content to oblige the democratic party to consider the possibility that their moral beliefs might have Christian roots. The analogy was designed to do that.

Tocqueville used the analogy to step outside the social conflicts of the transition from aristocracy to democracy. On the one hand, class conflicts had led aristocrats to use the Church in the defence of social privilege and political absolutism.

Religion has just for the moment become entangled with those institutions which democracy overturns, and so it is often brought to rebuff the equality it loves and to abuse freedom as its adversary, whereas by taking it by the hand it could sanctify its efforts.   (*OC* Ia. 9)

At the same time class conflicts had blinded the democratic party to the moral beliefs required for self-government. 'They have seen religion in the ranks of their adversaries and that is enough for them; some of them openly attack it, and the others do not dare to defend it.'

If the moral incoherence created by class conflict had so far prevented France from finding a new consensus, the analogy between Christian morality and civil equality suggested a way forward. By arguing in this way Tocqueville followed a path which had been cleared by Protestant liberals under the Restoration. They had detached Christianity from proprietary claims made by Catholic reactionaries, who presented democracy as deeply subversive of Christianity. At the same time, these Protestants had detached liberalism from philosophical materialism and utilitarian morals. Thus, Tocqueville's association of a rights-based theory of justice with religious imagery was carefully premeditated. The sight of religious men opposing liberty—'where the love of order is confused with a taste for oppression, and the *holy cult of freedom* with a contempt of law'—he found repugnant. Equally, he detested those who used liberty chiefly to attack religion: 'Others speak of liberty as if they were able to feel its sanctity and its majesty and loudly demand for humanity those rights which they have always refused to acknowledge' (*OC* Ia. 10).

The analogy between Christian morality and civil equality became the cornerstone of Tocqueville's argument in *Democracy in America* (1835). That emerges in the earliest chapters. In order to explain how the Americans had become a self-governing people, Tocqueville was obliged to decide upon the relative importance of three factors shaping their social condition: the physical circumstances of the North American continent; the *mœurs* of the original settlers, their 'point of departure'; and the role of positive laws. Letters he wrote during his first months in America—when travelling from New York to the Michigan wilderness and then from French Canada to New England—reveal a debate within his mind about the relative importance of these factors. The conclusions he reached shaped the early chapters of the book.

Immediately after describing the physical circumstances of North America, the unlimited opportunities a fertile and almost empty continent provided for the European settlers, Tocqueville turns his attention to the 'point of departure of the Anglo-Americans'—the attitudes and habits, or *mœurs*, which the settlers of New England brought from the mother country. Drawn from the English middle classes and moved by a Protestantism almost republican in its emphasis on equality, these settlers carried with them attitudes and habits fostered by local autonomy in England. They were used to meeting, debating, and settling local affairs. And, as a matter of course, they drew on those attitudes and habits in founding their colonies. Thus, social equality and the sovereignty of the people grew up together in New England.

Their gathering on American soil offered, from the outset, the singular phenomenon of a society in which there were neither great lords nor common people, neither rich nor poor . . . And while the hierarchy of rank despotically classed the inhabitants of the mother country, the colony approximated more and more to the novel spectacle of a community homogeneous in all its parts. A democracy more perfect than antiquity had

51

dared to dream of issued in full size and panoply from the midst of an ancient feudal society. (*OC* Ia. 31–4)

Their profound religious beliefs and political habits—'communal self-government, that germ or powerful source of free institutions, had already entered deeply into English habits'—set the New England settlers apart from other colonists (*OC* Ia. 28). Other colonies had been established by adventurers, by men without fortune or education. By contrast, the middle-class settlers of New England were moved by beliefs which sanctioned both social equality and self-government.

In New England, the analogy between Christian morality and civil equality sustained an alliance between the 'spirit of religion' and the 'spirit of liberty'. Instead of being at war, as they were in France, these two were joined in 'a marvellous combination'. The passage celebrating that combination reveals Tocqueville's chief hope in writing *Democracy in America* (1835).

Religion perceives in civil liberty a noble exercise for the faculties of man; and in the political world a field prepared by the Creator for the efforts of mind. Free and powerful in its own sphere, satisfied with the place reserved for it, religion never more surely establishes its empire than when it reigns in the hearts of man unsupported by anything save its native strength.

Liberty regards religion as its companion in all its battles and its triumphs, as the cradle of its infancy and the divine source of its rights. It considers religion as the safeguard of *mœurs*, and *mœurs* as the best security of law and the surest pledge of the duration of freedom. (*OC* Ia. 42–3)

Belief in the moral equality of men led to acceptance that freedom is a birthright, ruling out permanent social inequalities, and in that way religion and liberty became allies. The multiplicity of Christian sects in America only underlined the wide area of moral agreement.

In the Southern states, however, the point of departure was different. There 'no noble thought, no immaterial motives' had governed the establishment of new colonies. Moreover, the introduction of slavery in the Southern states brought the only approximation to aristocratic social conditions in the United States. 'Slavery dishonours work,' Tocqueville observed. 'It introduces idleness into society, and with it ignorance and pride, poverty and luxury. It degrades human intelligence and stifles human activity.' The triumph of free institutions in the United States never entirely effaced the difference in *mœurs* between New England and the Southern states, the difference in their 'point of departure'.

Tocqueville's reflections on the 'wonderful alliance' between the spirit of religion and the spirit of liberty in New England gave rise to his notion of free *mœurs*, the attitudes and habits of a people who rely on themselves and freely associate in order to deal with public needs as they emerge. Profound differences between American and French society obliged him to make a distinction not usually made by Restoration liberals; that is, he distinguished the social condition of a people from its *mœurs*, the passive from the active aspects of social structure. The former included civil law and the distribution of property, while the latter referred to the attitudes and habits that a people could carry with them into a radically new situation—just as the New England settlers had carried their free *mœurs* to the New World.

But what of the two other factors shaping American institutions, positive laws and physical circumstances? In discussing positive laws, Tocqueville concentrated less on formal equality before the law than on the laws governing inheritance—laws which, he argued, had a decisive influence on social structure through their effect on the distribution of property and the nature of the family. He devoted a chapter to arguing that neither France nor the United States exhibited the concentration of landed property which still made it possible to describe English society as aristocratic. Here the influence of the 1820s debate about primogeniture and entail is easiest to detect and, for once, that influence was slightly unfortunate. It led Tocqueville to exaggerate the importance of changes in the law of inheritance after the American Revolution. He was so anxious to establish the similarity of social condition between France and the United States, that he did not adequately notice the difference between laws *permitting* equal distribution of property among children and laws *enforcing* such equal distribution, the rule of 'equal shares' introduced in France by Napoleon's Civil Code.

In fact, Tocqueville's discussion of the physical circumstances of North America had already made it clear that, quite apart from the influence of laws, the concentration of landed property necessary for an aristocratic society was unlikely to develop. Vast tracts of unoccupied land and the possibility of moving West made labour too expensive for the development of great landed estates on the European model.

American soil repulsed completely a territorial aristocracy. It was soon obvious that to clear that rebellious terrain nothing less than the constant and interested efforts of the owner were needed. When that was done, the crops were not sufficient to enrich both a master and a farmer. Land thus came to be divided naturally into small properties that the owner alone cultivated. (*OC* Ia. 29)

But, if so, was it possible that physical circumstances were the decisive factor shaping American institutions—more important, that is, than either *mœurs* or laws? After leaving New York, when he first began to travel through the American wilderness, Tocqueville had asked himself that question. But it was his visit to French Canada which finally provided the answer, and enabled him to rank *mœurs*, laws, and physical circumstances in a definite order of causal importance.

What Tocqueville had observed in Quebec province did not appear directly in *Democracy in America* (1835). None the less, what he saw there led him to downgrade the importance of physical environment and even laws compared to *mœurs*. When he and Beaumont had begun to travel west from Albany through the sparsely settled forests of upper New York, and especially during their 'adventure' in the Michigan wilderness, Tocqueville had been tempted to think that the almost unlimited land—what Frederick Jackson Turner was later to call 'the Frontier Theory'—was the decisive factor shaping American institutions. But as he travelled up the St Lawrence, that hypothesis rapidly lost its plausibility, for he found in French Canada a people who utterly lacked the self-governing passion and commercial instincts of the Anglo-Americans. Yet they lived in the same physical milieu, and indeed since the British conquest of Canada had lived under similar laws.

French Canadians remained in their narrow band of settlement along the St Lawrence. They did not seize the opportunities offered by an unsettled continent, preferring their own hearths, families, and villages. That difference between settlers from the two nations had decided the fate of North America—it was to be dominated by the Anglo-Americans. As he left Quebec and travelled to New England, Tocqueville composed an essay to explore the reasons for that difference. In it he argued that the *mœurs* of the French Canadians still bore the mark of the excessive centralization of French government under the *ancien régime*. The government in Paris had tried to foresee and regulate everything in its colony, rather than leaving the colonists to look after themselves as the English (at least until the 1760s) had done. The English colonies flourished and expanded because their settlers fell back on habits and attitudes shaped by local autonomy in England. French colonists, on the other hand, were used to the tutorship of the state.

Tocqueville concluded that the free *mœurs* of the New England settlers had been decisive in shaping American institutions. He placed that conclusion near the end of *Democracy in America* (1835) 'The laws contribute more to the maintenance of a democratic republic in the United States than physical circumstances, and *mœurs* contribute more than the laws' (*OC* Ia. 319). That conclusion enabled him, in turn, to present American federalism—with its spheres of authority extending from the township through the states to the national government—as a formalizing of the free *mœurs* of the Americans. Moral consensus in America, the absence of conflict between aristocratic and democratic principles, meant that the self-governing habits of the American settlers had never been undermined by bitter class conflicts. Instead, their free *mœurs* had created a new form of the state.

The consequence of social equality joined to free *mœurs* for the distribution of authority in the United States was striking. It was embodied in what Americans understood by 'the sovereignty of the people'. Authority proceeded upwards from the earliest associations of settlers rather than descending downwards from a superior class (gradually forced, as in Europe, to cede that authority to a 'sovereign state', which continued to treat the population at large as dependants). The implication for French readers was that authority had not been transferred to the centre in order to destroy local aristocratic power.

In Boston, where he found a more intellectual society than elsewhere in America, Tocqueville explored the roots of local autonomy in America, the township system. It was here, in conversation with the historian Jared Sparks, the German publicist Francis Lieber, and others, that he put the question which was at the heart of his journey—how a political system could be contrived which reconciled central power with local autonomy. It is hardly surprising that he gave more attention to the township than to the Federal government. The French did not need instruction in the workings of central government. What they needed was a clear picture of the rules which sustained local autonomy and the benefits which might now be derived from it.

Yet the French also needed to learn how American federalism differed from earlier confederal forms of government—how the constitutional system created distinct spheres of authority. 'This Constitution, which at first glance one is tempted to confuse with previous federal constitutions, in fact rests on an entirely new theory, a theory that should be hailed as one of the great discoveries of political science of our time' (*OC* Ia. 159). Whatever the rights accorded previous confederal governments (such as Switzerland, the German Empire, and the Netherlands), the constituent states kept the right of executing general laws or gathering general taxes to themselves, with the result that either the stronger member state imposed its own will on the others or the confederal government became almost impotent. Such was not the case in the United States.

In America, the Union's subjects are not states but private citizens. When it wants to levy a tax, it does not turn to the government of Massachusetts, but to each inhabitant of Massachusetts. Former federal governments had to confront whole peoples, the Union confronts individuals. It does not borrow its power, but draws it from within. It has its own administrators, courts, officers of justice and army. (*OC* Ia. 160)

Thus, Tocqueville used the American constitutional system—with the help of the *Federalist Papers* (written in 1787–8 by James Madison, Alexander Hamilton, and John Jay, urging acceptance of the proposed Constitution) and one or two commentaries on the Constitution—to resolve uncertainties or ambiguities which had plagued earlier liberal calls for a new federalism.

An unprecedented role for the courts was crucial to the 'new political science' suggested by American federalism, since the judiciary, and especially the Supreme Court, were empowered not only to apply laws but to declare them unconstitutional. That power of review, enabling the Supreme Court to judge not only private citizens but the acts of states, the Congress, and the President, meant that the whole political system was subject to the notion of fundamental or constitutional law. Moreover, the final interpretation of that fundamental law belonged to the Supreme Court. In that way, the American political system introduced a constraint on popular majorities, especially through basic individual rights defined in the Constitution whilst at the same time it secured the unity of the nation by giving to a national tribunal the final say over conflicts of jurisdiction. Both features helped to create a political system or state which was liberal and decentralized, without being anarchical in the fashion of earlier confederations.

At the local level, the role of the courts was equally novel and important. Appeals to the courts—either grand juries or the ordinary state courts—made it possible to correct administrative errors and even to carry out acts of administration, making a bureaucratic hierarchy unnecessary. 'Thus, the election of administrative officials or their irremovability from office, the absence of an administrative hierarchy and the introduction of judicial means into local government, are the principal characteristics of American administration from Maine to the Floridas' (*OC* Ia. 82). After learning about the role of town meetings, the accountability of local officials to the courts between elections as well as the grand jury system, Tocqueville was able to suggest ways in which even a unitary European state might be decentralized.

Altogether, Tocqueville used the American township to revise the Restoration liberal idea of centralization, distinguishing 'governmental' from 'administrative' centralization and arguing that governmental centralization did *not* entail administrative centralization. It was that 'discovery' which provided the hope that, in future, democratic societies would be able to combine central power with local autonomy. Previous French discussions of centralization had usually confused the two and had concluded— wrongly—that decentralization would create small, competing sovereigns. But American federalism demonstrated that a unified legal system, a single structure of legal authority, was compatible with decentralized administration.

The New England township also enabled Tocqueville to demonstrate both the practical and moral benefits of sustaining local autonomy in a political system. One major practical benefit was the emergence of a new theory of interests in the United States. In Europe, when Tocqueville wrote, there were two competing theories of interests—one, dominated by Benthamite utilitarianism, saw the public interest as simply an aggregation of individual interests, while the other, associated with Rousseau, postulated an objective public interest knowable apart from the *de facto* preferences of individuals. Each of these fed on the other. Both ignored the range of interests which were intermediate between the individual and the association of all, namely the state. By contrast, Tocqueville used his account of American federalism to suggest the need for a theory of concentric interests, interests which fanned out from the individual but did not ignore the needs of groups and areas less inclusive than the whole or the state. Such a theory of concentric interests remedied a radical weakness of the individualist, proto-liberal model of society which had emerged in seventeenth-century Europe—a remedy in some ways analogous to arguments put forward by the German philosopher Hegel in his *Philosophy of Right* (1821).

The advantage of conceiving interests as a series of concentric circles—on the model of the American township, county, and states—was that it helped to create a threshold sense of justice in a population, a sense of justice which worked against theories appealing only to aggregate individual claims or the reified claims of all. It provided citizens with a list of important interests, a kind of check-list, which ought to be considered in matters of public policy. It was remarkable proof of the way a political system could help to educate and moralize its members, making them sensitive to the claims of justice. Taken together, the constitutional arrangements embodied in American federalism encouraged a conception of interests which has since been called pluralist. *Democracy in America* (1835) can indeed be seen as the seminal work for the emergence of a pluralist model of democracy, for Tocqueville turned the tacit pluralism of the *Federalist Papers* into a self-conscious programme by introducing the threat of majority tyranny drawn from the background of French class conflict—by making the equalizing of social conditions an imperative for constructing a political system which constrains the operation of the majority principle.

It has been argued that Tocqueville's fear of majority tyranny shows that he failed to understand how the American constitution made the emergence of nationwide majorities less likely by multiplying spheres of authority through federalism and the separation of powers. But that view hardly stands up to examination. When Tocqueville began to consider the threat of majority tyranny, he emphasized that he was thinking of the states, which were the chief organ of government at the time, the Federal Government being concerned chiefly with foreign affairs. Often state constitutions had not been constructed with the same foresight as the Federal Constitution—weakening executive power and undermining the independence of the judiciary through the election of judges. But that was not all. Tocqueville also chose to concentrate on the states when discussing the threat of majority tyranny because they made the analogy with France and other unitary European states more plausible. Federalism was not, he assumed, a luxury which major European states could afford.

When Tocqueville began to discuss the virtues and vices of democratic government in a general way, he was in no doubt that its greatest virtue was that it fostered respect for and confidence in the law—because people knew that they had made the law and could, if need be, change it. Thus, while an aristocratic government often displayed more skill and consistency in managing affairs, it was moved by a partial interest. 'Under aristocratic rule, public men have a class interest which, though it sometimes agrees with that of the majority, is more often distinct therefrom' (*OC* Ia. 244). The fact that the level of education and skill among aristocratic magistrates was higher than in a democracy—where the instincts of the public discouraged the ablest men from seeking office and often threw power into the hands of those willing to flatter—did not prevent democratic institutions from working overall for the happiness of the greatest number, while aristocratic magistrates often unconsciously worked for the advantage of one section of society.

Democracy in America *(1835)*

Widespread fear in Europe that the advent of democracy would spell permanent disorder and violence was mistaken. That was, once again, to confuse class hatreds of the transition from aristocracy to democracy with the workings of the latter when it was fully established. Thus, respect for individual rights played an enormously important role in American government, embodying the reciprocity which was the natural complement to the premiss of equality underlying democratic societies. Tocqueville noticed that, in contrast to Europe, there was no outcry against property in the United States. The reason was clear—'everyone, having some possession to defend, recognizes the right to property in principle'. The sub-division of property made it an institution of general advantage. The very comparisons which bred discontent in a residually aristocratic society such as England became a source of stability when social conditions were more equal. That also applied to the political system. 'Democratic government makes the idea of political rights penetrate right down to the least of citizens, just as the division of property puts the general idea of property rights within reach of all' (*OC* Ia. 249). Citizens became loath to attack the rights of others because they did not want their own to be jeopardized. Thus, both the subdivision of property and the spread of political rights made it likely that revolutions would become rare in democracies, in sharp contrast to the expectations of Europeans in Tocqueville's day.

Far from feeling that the law is their natural enemy, citizens of a democratic republic usually identify with it and feel they have a personal interest in obeying it. That sense of involvement in government has a crucial consequence for civil society, for it means that habits of discussion and co-operation which mark the former, pass over into the latter. The habit of political association breeds civil associations. Indeed, an almost feverish activity becomes characteristic of democracies, with endless proposals for change and improvement. The self-esteem which political rights confer on a citizen becomes the source of self-confidence when he turns his hand to commercial undertakings. 'In politics he takes a part in undertakings he had not thought of, and they give him a general taste for enterprise' (*OC* Ia. 254). Thus, an aptitude for innovation springs unintended from the workings of a democratic political system. 'Democracy does not give to people the most skilful government, but it does what the most skilful government is often impotent to create; it spreads throughout the social body a restless activity, superabundant strength, an energy which never otherwise exists and which, if circumstances are favourable, gives birth to miracles' (*OC* Ia. 255). That prodigious energy fostered by political liberty becomes, in turn, an important safeguard against majority tyranny.

Democratic governments, unless they embody precautions such as those taken by the American federalists, tend to make legislatures powerful at the expense of executive and judicial power, thus lending themselves to the unrestrained force of the majority principle. The legislative power of the majority is reinforced by its moral power, by the assumption that the interests of the greatest number must prevail over those of lesser numbers and that the majority opinion is the best judge of those interests. The consequence—which Tocqueville observed in many state governments in the United States—was greater instability in laws and administration than under aristocratic governments. The political system was subject to sudden, unrestrained movements of public opinion, and continuity of policy, a great potential virtue of aristocratic polities, was lost.

Yet the greatest danger attending a democratic form of government was not instability but the tyranny of the majority. Tyranny, he believed, is a danger inherent in any sovereign power, whether exercised by one, by a few or by the majority, but it is a danger which acquires a new intensity when backed by the apparent moral authority of the majority. That is why a new idea of the state was urgently needed, an idea no longer tied to the stipulation of unlimited sovereign right vested in one agency. Tocqueville dismissed the traditional notion of mixed government as a chimera. In his view, every society is dominated finally by one 'principle of action'—and just as England in the early nineteenth century remained unambiguously an aristocratic society, so the United States was dominated by the democratic principle. Hence the importance of establishing that sovereign power, even when invested in the majority and its representatives, does not have the right to command whatever it chooses.

There exists a general law which has been made or at least adopted not only by a majority of this or that people, but by the majority of all men. That is called justice. Justice therefore sets limits on the rights of any people. (*OC* Ia. 26)

The implication is clear: a political system must be constructed which introduces a series of restraints on the unfettered rule of the majority. A bicameral legislature, an executive with some power of initiative and restraint as well as an independent judiciary are needed. But they are not enough.

The virtue of the American political system was that it suggested other types of restraint on the majority principle. If full-blown federalism is not possible (and, as we have seen, Tocqueville agreed it was not an option for European states surrounded by powerful rivals), then at least administrative decentralization is necessary to ensure that a passing national mood or opinion cannot be transmitted easily into action at every point and at the same moment. 'When the central government which represents it [i.e. a national majority] has given a sovereign order, it must rely, for the execution of its command, on agents who often do not depend upon it and which it cannot direct at will' (*OC* Ia. 224). Nor is that all. The unprecedentedly powerful role which the American political system gave to courts—the right to overturn legislative and executive acts in the name of fundamental or constitutional law—turns the whole legal class into a quasi-aristocratic body. For it gives lawyers an interest in limiting majority power, which is reinforced by the nature of legal education, especially when it turns on precedents in the fashion of Anglo-American common law. 'I am sure that in a society where lawyers occupy without opposition the elevated position which naturally belongs to them, their attitude will be eminently conservative and will reveal itself as anti-democratic' (*OC* Ia. 276). In the absence of princes and nobles, lawyers become the nearest thing to an aristocracy available.

The jury system provided still another restraint on the majority principle in America, only this time a form of self-restraint. For when the jury is considered not so much as a judicial institution, but as a political institution, it is clear that it tends 'to place the direction of society in the hands of the governed or a portion of them, and not in that of the rulers' (*OC* Ia. 284). For that reason, it is a deeply republican institution even in an aristocratic society such as England. It makes all or part of the people the final judge and, by introducing people to the rules and procedures of a legal system, it also has an important moralizing influence. It helps citizens to understand what is involved in applying legal rules to particular cases, and makes them aware of the nature and importance of legal rights.

The jury serves incredibly to form the judgment and increase the natural intelligence of a people. That, in my opinion, is its greatest advantage. One must consider it as a free and always open school, where every juror comes to learn about his rights, where he enters into daily communication with the most educated and enlightened of the upper classes, where laws are taught to him in a practical fashion. (*OC* Ia. 286)

By turning citizens into temporary magistrates, it not only develops their powers of judgement, but brings home to them the need to be responsible for their own actions and inculcates respect for the law—an attitude which is the last restraint against tyranny in a democratic society.

Three general features of the political system thus helped to minimize the threat of majority tyranny in the United States. First, the federal form of government which 'permits the union to enjoy the power of a great republic and the security of a small one'; secondly, the strength of communal institutions which keeps the tyranny of the majority at bay, giving people an aptitude for self-government; and thirdly, the role of the courts in restraining exaggerated movements of public opinion. Behind even these features lay the free *mœurs* of the Americans, sustained by that alliance of the 'spirit of liberty', and 'spirit of religion' which turned religion itself into an important political institution, through the respect for individual rights it inculcated and the restraint on majority opinion it thereby created.

If Tocqueville considered the influence of *mœurs* to be decisive in the long run, central to the shaping of American *mœurs* was a 'democratic and republican' form of Christianity. In America the belief that religion sanctioned civil equality or 'equal liberty' was universal. Moral consensus did not only provide a domestic haven from the agitations of political and commercial life, it also ensured that Americans carried a respect for basic rights into the public sphere which constrained both their thoughts and actions. Those who militated for change in America were obliged to 'show a certain respect for Christian morality and equity, which does not allow them to violate easily the laws when they obstruct the execution of their designs', he noticed (*OC* Ia. 306). 'Until now no one in the United States has dared to advance this maxim: that everything is permitted in the interest of society, an impious maxim that seems to have been invented in a century of liberty to legitimate all the tyrants to come.' Thus, by anchoring a respect for fundamental rights, religion in America became the most basic of all political institutions through its influence on *mœurs*. In America it was universally accepted that 'belief is necessary for the maintenance of republican institutions.'

Tocqueville was creating a salutary myth. The moralizing potential of political participation was the aspect of American decentralization that had taken him unawares—and which, by the time he visited Boston, had aroused his unfeigned admiration. The need and opportunity to do things together in a township created a sense of mutual concern and civic spirit. It demonstrated that a political system could moralize people, through participation in the making and execution of public decisions. Restoration liberals such as Constant and Barante had envisaged the practical advantages of local autonomy, but, above all, they had been concerned, in the tradition of Montesquieu, with dispersing power and creating a new political class or 'élite'. American institutions now persuaded Tocqueville that the moralizing potential of political participation was just as important. Indeed, he began to see the civic spirit fostered by local autonomy as the final guarantee against encroachment by a remote, tutelary power, a bureaucratic form of the state.

Administrative tidiness or uniformity of behaviour should not be confused with social vitality, yet that is what apologists for French administrative centralization confused.

I see most French communes, whose accounting system is excellent, plunged in profound ignorance of their true interests and overtaken by such invincible apathy that society there seems to vegetate rather than live; on the other hand, I see in America townships, with their untidy budgets lacking all uniformity, an enlightened, active and enterprising population . . . This contrast astonishes me, for to my mind the object of good government is to ensure the welfare of a people and not to establish a certain order in the midst of their misery. (*OC* Ia. 92–3, n. 51)

It was necessary to look beneath the surface to perceive the real effects of excessive centralization.

It is true that centralization can easily succeed in imposing an external uniformity on men's behaviour and that this uniformity comes to be loved for itself without reference to its objectives, just as the pious may adore a statue, forgetting the divinity it represents. Centralization can regulate the details of social control skilfully; check slight disorders and petty offences; and keep society in that state of administrative somnolence which administrators are in the habit of calling good order and public tranquillity. In a word, it excels at preventing, not at doing. (*OC* Ia. 91)

In America the absence of uniform rules and surface order could be a nuisance or worse. But the social and moral advantages resulting from administrative decentralization far outweighed such inconveniences.

The benefits were nothing less than vastly increased social vitality and the creation of self-reliant, energetic characters— citizens in the full sense of the word. Both were compromised, sooner or later, by excessive centralization.

In America the social force behind the state is much less well regulated, less enlightened, and less wise, but it is a hundred times more powerful than in Europe. Without doubt there is no other country on earth where people make such great efforts to achieve social prosperity. I know of no other people who have founded so many schools or such efficient ones, or churches more in touch with the religious needs of the inhabitants, or municipal roads better maintained. So it is no good looking in the United States for perfection of administrative procedures, what one does find is a picture of power, somewhat wild perhaps, but robust, and a life liable to mishaps but full of striving and animation. (*OC* Ia. 92)

The contrast with France was shaming. In France, so-called citizens were often totally alienated from the government of their country, reduced to little more than farm labourers. That was how administrative centralization proved to be the deadly enemy of citizenship. Far too often the Frenchman considered that 'the condition of his village, the policing of his road, and the repair of his church and parsonage do not concern him,' Tocqueville observed sadly. 'He thinks that all those things have nothing to do with him, but belong to a powerful stranger called the government' (*OC* Ia. 93).

Nor was that all. An overcentralized form of the state compromised not only citizenship but free will and morality itself.

What good is it to me, after all, if there is an authority always busy to see to the tranquil enjoyment of my pleasures and going ahead to brush all dangers away from my path without giving me even the trouble to think about it, if that authority, which protects me from the smallest thorns on my journey, is also the absolute master of my liberty and of my life? . . . What I admire most in America is not the administrative but the political effects of decentralization. In the United States the motherland's presence is felt everywhere. It is a subject of concern to the village and to the whole Union. The inhabitants care about each of their country's interests as if it were their own . . . He has much the same feeling for his country as one has for one's family; and a sort of selfishness makes him care for the state . . . Often to a European a public official stands for force; to an American he stands for right. It is therefore fair to say that a man never obeys another man, but justice, or the law.   (*OC* Ia. 93–5)

By analysing the advantages of local autonomy Tocqueville reached the highest ground of modern political theory. He was examining nothing less than the conditions of public morality and the problems posed by the scale of the modern nation-state. He was taking up issues raised by Jean-Jacques Rousseau in the previous century.

In *The Social Contract* (1762) Rousseau had attempted to identify the conditions in which it might be said that a man in obeying the law or the state was obeying himself—that is, his enlightened will—alone. Drawing heavily on the classical republican tradition, Rousseau concluded that, strictly speaking, the individual's will and what justice required could only be fused in a small-scale community where taking part in public debate and decision-making would result in citizens' wills becoming enlightened or moralized. (Indeed, Rousseau's concept of the 'General Will' introduced that fusion by definition). A large-scale state, even if endowed with representative institutions such as England enjoyed in the eighteenth century, could not achieve that goal, Rousseau argued. For wills cannot be represented. The shaping of intentions is possible only through direct participation in government, in public debate and decision-making.

We cannot be certain how familiar Tocqueville was with Rousseau's work, but it seems likely that he had *The Social Contract* in mind when he penned the above lines. His passion for civic virtue always had a strong ring of Rousseau. On the other hand, Tocqueville had been immersed in Restoration liberal writing directed at Rousseau's 'mistakes', or 'exaggerations'. For liberals like Madame de Staël and Constant had been at pains to point out that Rousseau succeeded in fusing individual intentions with justice only by means of definition—and, worse, by providing a formula which could be manipulated by a centralized power claiming to represent the General Will or 'the people'.

To liberals such as Constant, Rousseau's argument, which had been abused during the Reign of Terror, involved a confusion between 'virtue' and choice, between morality and liberty. Constant warned against the eighteenth-century enthusiasm for the *polis* and for the ancient definition of liberty as involving only participation. That definition failed to allow for the most important modern sense of the word, Constant argued, which was an area of private choice or autonomy, protected by civil rights. The moralizing potential of political participation had acquired a bad name as a result of the Reign of Terror. Hence Restoration liberals distrusted the rhetoric of civic humanism, and preferred to explore the means of representative government *à l'anglaise*.

Tocqueville became an exception to that trend. His earliest letters, as well as his Italian journal of 1826–7, breathed the spirit of ancient liberty or civic virtue. In a passage of that journal, reminiscent of Gibbon, Tocqueville dated the decline of Rome from the day in which the Roman Republic lost its liberty—that is, when the Empire destroyed free institutions. It may be significant that Hervé de Tocqueville, in a speech of the 1820s, warned against adolescent enthusiasm for classical republican institutions. He may have been thinking of his youngest son.

What took Tocqueville beyond the confines of Restoration liberalism were his reflections on the New England township and the opportunities it offered for participation within a nation-state. The American township enabled Tocqueville to 'save' part of Rousseau's defence of participation and its moralizing effects, while disregarding those aspects which ignored the differences between ancient and modern society, between the *polis* and the nation-state, between public virtue and private rights.

Tocqueville established that civic virtue could not mean the same thing in a modern democratic society as in the ancient *polis*. The unprecedented equality of status which distinguished modern Western societies from their predecessors had two crucial consequences—first, that every individual had the right to manage his life in affairs which concerned him alone; and, secondly, that every individual also had the need to do so. Such a right and such a need meant that the ancient concept of civic virtue, which presupposed a privileged class, could no longer serve, unrevised, as a standard. The dedication of a privileged, leisured class to the pursuit of 'glory' for the *polis*— a pursuit with strongly military connotations—had to make way for the essentially commercial, private activities which equality opened up to individuals in a democratic society. Now every individual had to look after his own affairs, as well as concern himself with public matters. Therefore the highest standard of morality in a society of equals is 'enlightened self-interest', a conception of one's own interests which takes account of the equal basic rights of others. Appeals to public virtue—to the disciplines of citizenship—become an abuse if they threaten justice or equal rights, if they subordinate the private sphere unduly. By making that clear, with the help of American constitutionalism, Tocqueville was able to put forward an unambiguously liberal doctrine of citizenship.

Tocqueville resurrected the ideal of civic spirit by demonstrating that it could be combined with a liberal conception of justice. But not only that. He also demonstrated that a decentralized form of the state had a major role to play in fostering and sustaining civic spirit, especially in societies which had become democratic by centralizing power to destroy aristocratic privilege. While travelling through the United States in September 1831, he wrote in a notebook that 'in America, free *mœurs* have created free institutions; in France, free institutions must create free *mœurs*.' It was to be the theme of *Democracy in America* (1835).

4 *Democracy in America* (1840)

Democracy in America (1840) took far more time to write than Tocqueville had expected. But that is hardly surprising. For it is bold and original. It requires so much of the reader's imagination that it did not have the immediate popular success of its 1835 predecessor. None the less, it is the book which guarantees Tocqueville's reputation as a social thinker, for here he is on his own ground and constantly innovating. The framework of argument he had taken over from Restoration liberalism still provides the background, but within that framework Tocqueville does things no social thinker had previously attempted.

The focus of *Democracy in America* (1840) is not primarily political, though in the last section Tocqueville returns to the themes of his earlier book. For the most part, he is concerned to explore the influence of two types of society, aristocratic and democratic, on ideas, feelings, and habits—that is, on *mœurs*. Such a project was original enough. But the manner in which Tocqueville executes it is even more so. He moves decisively beyond the confines of eighteenth-century proto-sociology, beyond the methods of Montesquieu and writers of the Scottish Enlightenment. These writers had identified different types of society by examining a range of practices which, taken together, made up a social structure. It was the way in which these practices 'fitted together' which had fascinated Montesquieu and the eighteenth-century Scots. Their point of view was external and the type of explanation they offered was causal explanation, in Hume's sense of observable regularities of behaviour.

But Tocqueville is not satisfied with a merely external or behavioural point of view. He wants to grasp what is going on from within, to understand what it is like to act in each type of society. How is the meaning of action shaped by aristocratic and democratic social conditions? In order to find out, Tocqueville constructs imaginary agents typical of each society—'aristocratic man' and 'democratic man'—by drawing on meanings available in the beliefs and practices of that society. In the 1840 *Democracy in*

America, therefore, reasons for acting loom at least as large as causal explanations.

In effect, Tocqueville invites his readers to become actors—to read scripts for agents typical of each society and to notice how those scripts conjure up different imaginings, feelings, and intentions with each script leading the reader into a different self. In that way, Tocqueville is able to demonstrate that aristocratic and democratic societies correspond to different types of human agent.

The originality of Tocqueville's method has seldom been noticed. Yet it represented a breakthrough in social thought. For it pointed the way beyond a dilemma which had come to plague social thought and which plagues it still. Tocqueville's method combines forms of explanation usually presented as alternatives—causal or behavioural explanation on the one hand, explanation by appeal to reasons for acting on the other. He explores aristocratic and democratic societies by moving between observable social practices and the motives of typical agents, showing how each influences the other. In his account, the imagination becomes a crucial intermediary, reflecting social conditions and yet contributing to intentions which can alter those conditions.

Just how did Tocqueville come to argue in this way? Different philosophical traditions lay behind his method and that of the Scottish Enlightenment. For in Tocqueville's writings the influence of British empiricism, with its reliance on causal explanation, is offset by the influence of a French tradition which emphasized introspection. Rousseau's conception of liberty serves to illustrate the difference between the two philosophical traditions. Rousseau found the empiricist definition of liberty—as the absence of obstacles or impediments to movement—too external and physical to capture the nature of human choice. He argued that what distinguishes men from animals is their capacity to choose the rules which govern their actions, to bend their wills to a rule. The intentional character of human action distinguishes it from animal behaviour.

For French philosophers such as Rousseau, therefore, social institutions became not so much patterns of behaviour as sets of rules to be followed. That concern for an interior dimension, so prized by the French and so neglected by British empiricists, reemerges in Tocqueville's method, and helps him to identify a necessary connection between social practices and personal intentions. Indeed, by joining empiricist and introspective forms of explanation, Tocqueville's method suggests that relying merely on one or the other creates a false dilemma for social thought— confining it either to an 'external' or an 'internal' vantage-point, when the real need is to explore the interaction of social conditions and personal intentions. They must be examined side by side. For they are two sides of the same coin.

Tocqueville had, to be sure, little taste for formal philosophy. But it does not follow that he was uninfluenced by philosophical developments in France under the Restoration. A new emphasis on the will, on active or voluntary experience, was the hallmark of a group of philosophers which included Royer-Collard, Maine de Biran, and Victor Cousin. Maine de Biran, the most original and influential of the group, criticized eighteenth-century empiricism for denaturing the idea of causation—for holding up a model of causation which excluded reasons or beliefs as causes. In his view, willing or acting with intent was the *source* of our idea of a real relation between events. By contrast, the relations between events which empiricism postulated on the basis of external observation—what it called 'causal relations'—were merely hypothetical and parasitic on our experience of willing and acting. Biran concluded that experience of ourselves as agents was *sui generis*. It could not be reduced to involuntary, externally 'caused' experience. These 'two facts' of experience were equally fundamental and required different modes of explanation.

At the outset of the Restoration Maine de Biran was the centre of a philosophical group which included Guizot, who began in the 1820s to use Biran's emphasis on 'two modes' of experience to write a new kind of history, one in which analysis of changes in social structure alternated with intellectual history, analysis of changes in ideas or beliefs.

It is clear that the history of civilization could be treated in two fashions, drawn from two sources, considered under two different aspects. The historian could place himself inside the human soul, during a given period, a series of centuries or with a given people. He could study, describe, narrate all the events, all the transformations or revolutions which had taken place in the interior of man. And when he had finished, he would have a history of civilization for the people and the period he had chosen. He could proceed in another way: instead of entering into the interior of man, he could place himself outside. He could place himself in the midst of the events of the world. Instead of describing the vicissitudes of the ideas and sentiments of the individual being, he can describe external facts, events, changes in social structure. These two portions, these two histories of civilization are intimately joined to one another. They are the reflection, the image of each other. (Guizot, *History of Civilization in Europe*, 1828, 29)

In that way Guizot turned Maine de Biran's critique of eighteenth-century empiricism—with its insistence on the 'two facts' of experience, and the consequent need for two types of explanation—into a new model for social explanation. Tocqueville took on that model when immersing himself in Guizot's writings in the late 1820s. It shaped his method, though he probably remained unaware of his debt to Maine de Biran.

Tocqueville had learned to use this method in the 1835 *Democracy in America*. There his discussion of the law of inheritance revealed a dual approach.

The law of equal distribution [among children] proceeds by two methods: by acting upon things, it acts upon persons; by influencing persons, it affects things; by both these means the law succeeds in striking at the root of landed property, and dispersing rapidly both family and fortunes. (*OC* Ia. 49)

Tocqueville did not formalize his method, still less did he put it forward as the basis for a new 'science of society'. He wrote before professional intellectual life created such temptations, simply wanting to understand as much as he could about two types of society. None the less, Tocqueville's way of exploring the interaction of social conditions and personal intentions, as well as his open concern to defend liberty, may have had an important influence on later social thought. Certainly, it is striking how the late nineteenth-century German sociologist Max Weber's recommendations for social explanation incorporate the above features. Weber may have grasped that Tocqueville's method offered a way to get beyond the conflict between positivism and idealism, 'causes' and 'reasons'—a dilemma which the German philosophical tradition had created in an acute form.

In any case, Tocqueville's method enabled him to explore the socializing process in aristocratic and democratic societies in a strikingly original way—that is, by comparing typical agents in each. His method immediately makes it clear that aristocratic and democratic societies are internally related to quite different conceptions of liberty. In the former, liberty is understood under the guise of 'privileges'; in the latter, it is understood as a general right, as enjoining 'equal liberty'.

Those different understandings of liberty provide the key to the different ways in which personal identity is formed in aristocratic and democratic societies. In an aristocratic society, freedom is not really a moral principle but a social rank: identity or rank in a society founded on privilege is assigned at birth. Some are born with a right to command, others with a duty to obey. There is no social role shared equally by all. Strictly speaking, there are no individuals in such a society. It is pre-individualist because beliefs and practices do not rest on the assumption of a shared or 'human' nature, on the assumption of 'natural' equality.

When the conditions of men are very unequal and the inequalities are permanent, individuals become little by little so dissimilar that each class assumes the aspect of a distinct race. . . . The most profound and capacious minds of Rome and Greece were never able to reach the idea, at once so general and so simple, of the common likeness of men and of the common birthright of each to freedom; they tried to prove that slavery was in the order of nature and that it would always exist. . . . All the great writers of antiquity belonged to the aristocracy of masters, or at least they saw that aristocracy established and uncontested before their eyes. Their mind, after it had expanded in several directions, was barred from further progress in this one, and the advent of Jesus Christ upon earth was required to teach that all the members of the human race are by nature equal and alike. (OC Ib. 22)

An aristocratic conception of liberty, freedom understood as a privilege, is the natural expression of a society in which unequal identities are assigned at birth.

That is why it is misleading to speak of 'individuals' in an aristocratic society. Members of the different castes have nothing in common and scarcely see themselves as belonging to the same species. Such extreme social inequality has important consequences for the nature and extent of sympathy.

Democracy in America *(1840)*

With an aristocratic people, each caste has its own opinions, feelings, rights, customs, and modes of living. Thus the men who compose it do not resemble all of the others; they do not think or feel in the same manner, and they scarcely believe that they belong to the same race. They cannot, therefore, thoroughly understand what others feel, nor judge of others by themselves. (*OC* Ib. 171–2)

The sympathy uniting members of a caste is lively and powerful, but outside its ranks such sympathy scarcely exists. That is just what the progress of social equality changes. 'When all the ranks of a community are nearly equal, as all men think and feel nearly in the same manner, each of them may judge in a moment the sensations of all the others; he casts a rapid glance upon himself and that is enough.' As a result democratic man can readily enter into almost any form of suffering. 'It does not really matter that strangers or even foes are the sufferers, imagination immediately puts him in their place' (*OC* Ib. 174). Thus social equality tends to give sympathy a universal compass. It is now one individual sympathizing with other individuals. In that sense, equality before the law brings 'the individual' into being as a publicly acknowledged or social role. It extends the range of sympathy, while reducing its intensity—which is why democratic ages tend to be rational and philanthropic, while aristocratic ages are passionate and unjust.

Because a democratic society rests on the postulate of civil equality, it introduces an attribute shared equally by all, and that, in turn, has an important consequence for personal identity. In a caste society, where status is assigned at birth and retained through life, a person's rank *constitutes* his identity; there is no basis in beliefs and practices for drawing a distinction between 'the individual' and the roles he or she may occupy. But in a democratic society the foundation of personal identity changes. Civil equality makes it necessary to distinguish between the individual and roles he or she may occupy, for these roles no longer exhaust personal identity. Tocqueville's argument implies that in a democratic society all roles become secondary in relation to the universal or primary role—that of the individual, which is, by definition, shared equally by all.

That change in the agent's relations with him or herself means that whereas identities in an aristocratic society seem 'natural' or fated, in a democratic society they are constructed or artificial. For comparison is the essence of a democratic society. Individuals can distinguish between persons and roles, compare roles and aspire (at least in principle) to almost any role. That yields a remarkable result—there is an unprecedented release of energy in a democratic society. Individuals are no longer held back by fixed or assigned identities. They can aspire to power, wealth, and status. Thus, civil equality fosters a society marked by ambition, innovation and restlessness. When people no longer feel tied to a particular situation, they compare what they have with what they might have, and the consequence is the multiplication of wants. Instead of the static wants of an aristocratic society, where people feel that their lot is fixed, members of a democratic society are obsessed with acquiring what they do not yet have.

In discussing the multiplication of wants, Tocqueville takes up a phenomenon which had fascinated Adam Smith and other eighteenth-century Scots. But his treatment is quite different from theirs. Instead of identifying the function such increased wants have in forwarding economic growth and the division of labour, Tocqueville explores the effect on the individual self or soul. He contrasts the type of personality fostered by a caste society with its fixed positions and by a democratic society with its apparently unbounded prospects.

In certain areas of the Old World . . . the inhabitants are for the most part extremely ignorant and poor; they take no part in the business of the country and are frequently oppressed by the government, yet their countenances are generally placid and their spirits light. In America I saw the freest and most enlightened men placed in the happiest circumstances that the world affords; it seemed to me that a cloud habitually hung upon their brows, and I thought them serious and almost sad, even in their pleasures. The chief reason for this contrast is that the former do not think of the ills they endure, while the latter are forever brooding over the advantages they do not possess. (*OC* Ib. 142)

Thus, if the release of ambition and multiplication of wants is one aspect of greater equality, the other is disappointment and frustration. The terrible restlessness of a democratic society springs from both of these things, from the hopes it generates and then dashes.

Democracy in America *(1840)*

When all the privileges of birth and fortune are abolished, when all professions are open to all, and a man's own energies may place him at the top of any one of them, an easy and boundless career seems open to his ambition and he can easily persuade himself that he is born to no common destiny. But this is an erroneous notion which is corrected by daily experience. The same equality which allows every citizen to conceive these lofty hopes renders all the citizens less able to realize them. It circumscribes their powers on every side, while it gives freer scope to their desires. They have swept away the privileges of some of their fellow creatures which stood in their way, but they have opened the door to universal competition. (*OC* Ib. 144)

The moral cost of a society in which everyone is subject to market relations—for here Tocqueville describes the hopes and fears intrinsic to what the eighteenth-century Scots called a market economy—is high. Tocqueville's aristocratic background makes him sensitive to the price exacted by social equality: 'to these causes must be attributed that strange melancholy which often haunts the inhabitants of democratic countries in the midst of their abundance, and that disgust of life which sometimes seizes upon them in the midst of . . . their easy existence' (*OC* Ib. 145). By contrast, in an aristocratic society a kind of serenity and even gaiety can be traced to people knowing exactly who they are. They are not subject to the torments of unsatisfied ambition.

A paradox results. Aristocratic societies, apparently so immobile, foster a wide range of tastes, passions and prejudices among their differently placed members. But a democratic society, for all the energy it unleashes and the restless activity which mark it, casts nearly all ambitions in the same mould, a commercial mould. Everyone is exposed to the pressures of the market-place, and calculations of utility are therefore imposed. The pursuit of wealth becomes an almost universal passion, when there are no longer fixed social positions which support other passions, noble and ignoble. In that sense, while a democratic society fosters ambition, the commercial character of that ambition makes it 'mediocre'— calculations of cost and benefit necessarily constrain and shape aspiration.

As a democratic society involves the formal separation of its members, they are no longer born into permanent associations or corporations. Rather, they are bound to stand on their own feet and make choices. For that reason the development of social equality is paralleled by the increasing importance of the idea of contract. Contract rather than assigned status becomes the key to social relations in one sphere after another. If an aristocratic society imposes obligations without admitting choice—so that the obligations cannot, strictly, be called moral—a democratic society tends to present all obligations as self-imposed. In the former case the bonds holding people together are almost tangible, while in the latter case such ties are necessarily abstract and conditional, less real than the individual will which brings them into being and can abrogate them.

Tocqueville's 'dual' method works nowhere with greater effect than here. He is able to show how, in a democratic society, greater fragility of personal identity is reflected in greater fragility of association. We have seen that whereas aristocratic man can 'enjoy' his assigned identity, democratic man is constantly in search of his. The first knows who he is, the second is far from sure. That difference accounts for the potential moral superiority of a democratic society. But it is also a potential weakness. For, if the burden of choice becomes too great—if the multiplication of wants results chiefly in disappointment—then the role for choice created by civil equality may result in a despair and passivity more dangerous than the pride and deference of an aristocratic society. It may result in what Tocqueville calls 'democratic envy', a combination of resentment and fear which threatens the habit of association.

In ceasing to be corporate—that is, made up of hereditary associations—a democratic society throws individuals into a competitive situation. Whatever the *de facto* pressures of survival and work, the only associations to which they necessarily belong are the state on the one hand (the source of their formally equal standing), and the 'natural' association of the family on the other. Thus, the usual basis for association is voluntary. That is both the strength and the weakness of a democratic society, for if the release of ambition is outweighed by disappointment—or, worse still, class resentments during the transition from aristocracy to democracy—there is a danger that the process of comparison will get out of hand and 'democratic envy' make everyone the enemy of his neighbour. If so, an excessive privatizing of life weakens the habit of association, the formal separation of the members of a democratic society then turns into a real dissociation, with disastrous political consequences.

Even the natural association of the family reflects this change in the structure of society, the new importance of voluntary association. For the family is a microcosm. In an aristocratic society the father and the eldest son are raised above the other members, while in a democratic society paternal authority is much reduced and only temporary.

In America the family in the Roman and aristocratic signification of the word, does not exist. All that one finds of it are a few vestiges in the first years of childhood, when the father exercises without opposition that absolute domestic authority which the feebleness of its children renders necessary and which their first interest, as well as his own incontestable superiority, warrants. But as soon as the young American approaches manhood, the ties of filial obedience are relaxed day by day; master of his thoughts, he is soon master of his conduct.

Among aristocratic nations social institutions recognize, in truth, no one in the family but the father; children are received by society at his hands; society governs him, he governs them. He is the author and the support of his family. Thus the parent has not only a natural right. He acquires a political right to command them, he is their author and the support of his family; but he is also its constituted ruler. (*OC* Ib. 201)

In democratic societies the principle of equal liberty holds such sway that children are liberated without opposition from the father. Civil equality transforms the relationship between the family and political authorities. In aristocratic societies the 'government never makes a direct appeal to the mass of the governed; as men are united together, it is enough to lead the foremost, the rest will follow'. But democratic social conditions make the idea of such an intermediary repugnant.

Social conditions thus operate through their influence on the imagination. 'While most of the conditions of life are extremely unequal and the inequality of those conditions is permanent, the notion of a superior grows upon the imagination of men; even if the law invested him with no privileges, custom and public opinion would concede them.' Democratic social conditions, by contrast, give the imagination quite a different bias. 'When, on the contrary, men differ but little from each other and do not always remain in different conditions of life, the general notion of a superior becomes weaker and less distinct. It is then vain for legislation to strive to place him who obeys very much below him who commands; for the *mœurs* of the time bring the two men nearer to one another, and draw them daily towards the same level' (*OC* Ib. 202). Does society gain from these changes in the family? Tocqueville is inclined to think that while the decline in the authority of the father may weaken the family as a unit, it allows more relaxed and affectionate relations among its members to develop.

Equally striking is the change in the relationship between master and servant, a change symptomatic of new conditions of work as gradations of rank disappear from society. Tocqueville emphasizes that a democratic society is consistent with there being richer and poorer classes. But it alters significantly the nature of their relations.

In aristocratic societies not only are the classes of servants and masters permanently separated from each other; each has many gradations of rank within it. The principle of hierarchy shapes everything. The result is a curious intimacy in the relations between persons who are formally superiors and inferiors—the master coming to look upon his servants 'as an inferior and secondary part of himself, so that he often takes an interest in their lot by a last stretch of selfishness' (*OC* Ib. 187). The servants, in turn, come to identify themselves with their master 'so that they become an appendage to him in their own eyes as well as in his'. Condescension on the one hand, and pride on the other, join to produce a strange result. 'The servant ultimately detaches his notion of himself from his own person; he deserts himself as it were, or rather he transports himself into the character of his master and thus assumes an imaginary personality. He complacently invests himself with the wealth of those who command him; he enjoys their fame, exalts himself with their rank, and feeds his mind with borrowed greatness' (*OC* Ib. 188). Nothing like this can be found in democratic societies, where no one is born into a position of permanent superiority or inferiority.

Not only legal equality, but the fact of social mobility, prevent the rich and poor from coming to see themselves as essentially different in democratic societies.

Democracy in America *(1840)*

At any moment a servant may become a master, and he hopes to become so, the servant is therefore not a different man from the master. Why, then, has the former a right to command, and what compels the latter to obey except the free and temporary consent of both their wills? Neither of them is by nature inferior to the other; they only become so for a time by contract. Within the terms of this contract the one is a servant, the other a master; beyond it they are two citizens, two men. (*OC* Ib. 189)

The model of contract invades all spheres of work as gradations of rank disappear and along with them the hereditary corporations in which work was organized. In consequence, work loses its menial connotations. In the United States, the rehabilitation of work means that even the very rich have to appear to have a useful occupation—or else disappear to Europe, where they can find the remains of a leisured class.

Aristocratic and democratic social conditions influence the intellectual domain as well as practical life. In an aristocratic society generations and classes are bound tightly together. People inherit the beliefs and prejudices appropriate to their station, and are not disposed to challenge them. There is an instinctive defer-ence to authority. When servants obey their masters without hesitation, they perceive not just one man but the whole class of their superiors and the general fact of subordination imposes on inferiors' imaginations and opinions as well as their habits. Thus, the master not only 'commands their actions, to a certain extent he even directs their thoughts' (*OC* Ia. 187). But the disappearance of ranks in society changes all that.

In place of instinctive trust in authority comes an instinctive distrust of it. The right of private judgement—that right which had received formal philosophical definition by Descartes—is the natural corollary of democratic social conditions, claimed by people who have never studied Descartes or any philosophy.

Where the citizens are all placed on an equal footing and closely seen by one another, and where no signs of incontestable greatness or superiority are seen in any one of them, they are constantly brought back to their own reason as the most obvious and reliable source of truth. It is not only confidence in this or that man which is destroyed, but the disposition to trust the authority of any man whatsoever. Everyone shuts himself tightly within himself and insists on judging the world from there. (*OC* Ib. 18)

But that does not mean that freedom of thought is unlimited in a democratic society.

For any society to exist, and for its members to co-operate, some beliefs or opinions have to be taken as given; such beliefs or opinions act as a premiss for further thought and action. 'Men living in aristocratic ages are therefore naturally induced to shape their opinions by the standard of a superior person, or a superior class of persons, while they are averse to recognizing the infallibility of the mass of the people.' The opposite is true in a democratic society. For the more men become alike, the less inclined they are to place their trust in anyone more or less like themselves. Yet the confidence they withdraw from individuals, they place in the multitude, in the judgement of the public at large. 'The public, therefore, among a democratic people has singular power, which aristocratic nations cannot conceive; for it does not persuade others to its beliefs, but it imposes them and makes them permeate the thinking of everyone by the enormous pressure of the mind of all upon the intelligence of each' (*OC* Ib. 18).

In the 1840 *Democracy in America* Tocqueville is even more concerned with the 'tyranny of the majority' as a moral than a political threat. Contrasting the socializing process in aristocratic and democratic societies enables him to see how the transparency introduced by social equality—the ease with which individuals enter the minds of others, in contrast to the opaqueness resulting from the different opinions and prejudices of the castes in an aristocratic society—can lead to a dangerous abdication of private judgement. Individuals may lose confidence in their own ability to reason, if it leads to conclusions which differ from those universally held. The power of widely shared opinions unnerves them.

The result is a moral aberration. The fact that an opinion is widely shared leads to a conclusion that it ought to be accepted. That conclusion takes its toll of reasoned argument. Thus, moral and intellectual enfeeblement may result from individual judgements abdicating in the face of public opinion. In 1835 Tocqueville had castigated the 'courtier' spirit which makes individuals more supine before the democratic public than courtiers ever were before absolute monarchs.

In absolute governments the great nobles who are nearest to the throne flatter the passions of the sovereign and voluntarily truckle to his caprices. But the mass of the nation does not degrade itself by servitude; it often submits from weakness, from habit, or from ignorance. . . . There is a great difference between doing what one does not approve, and feigning to approve what one does; the one is the weakness of a feeble person, the other befits the temper of a lackey. In free countries, where everyone is more or less called upon to give his opinion on affairs of state . . . and where sovereign authority is accessible on every side and where its attention can always be attracted by vociferation, more persons are to be met with who speculate upon its weaknesses and live upon ministering to its passions than in absolute monarchies. (OC Ia. 268–9)

It is as if formal equality created a duty to share the opinions of the public, resulting not in independence of judgement but conformity, a pandering to opinions because they are widely shared.

Sadly, that threat of moral autonomy springs from the very equality which sanctions it, the formal separation of individuals in democratic society. But there is an antidote to the threat available. It can be overcome with the help of associations. For, by associating and discovering others who share an opinion, individuals acquire greater confidence in their own judgements. Together, they can improve their reasons for holding an opinion, and seek to persuade the public at large, especially through the medium of newspapers. 'The more equal the conditions of men become and the less strong men individually are, the more easily they give way to the current of a multitude and the more difficult it is for them to adhere by themselves to the opinions which the multitude discards.' However, a newspaper not only represents a partial association within the larger society, but constantly reinforces that association through discussion. 'It may be said to address each of its readers in the name of all the others and to exert its influence over them in proportion to their individual weakness' (OC Ib. 120–1). That is why the influence of the press must increase as social conditions are equalized. The press provides the necessary condition of association, and serves to develop particular points of view. It is through association that men acquire confidence in their own judgement and the habit of exercising that judgement. Thus, the multiplication of associations is the best antidote to conformity in a democratic society. Tocqueville was aware that in his own day those who defended an aristocratic model of society feared that greater social equality would lead to moral and intellectual anarchy. But that was not the danger he feared. Rather, he feared that moral and intellectual stagnation might result from the tyranny of public opinion, from the temptation to be guided by the opinions of others rather than one's own reason.

The great risk run by a democratic society is not too much moral autonomy, but not enough—not too much variety, but not enough. Aristocratic societies formerly gave a corporate basis to values such as the patriotism and love of display of a military aristocracy, the prudence of the bourgeoisie, the stoicism of the peasantry, the other-worldliness of the clergy at their best. These values or attitudes were, so to speak, permanently held up to society. They provided an inherent pluralism. But, by its nature, a democratic society ceases to provide a permanent institutional home for such values or attitudes. Instead, their espousal becomes a matter for individual choice. Their espousal has a new fragility, similar to the fragility of personal identity and of association in a democratic society.

In discussing the tyranny of the majority as a moral threat, Tocqueville developed an argument he had met in Guizot's lectures in the 1820s. Guizot had argued that the progressive character of European civilization (when compared to the relatively stagnant character of other civilizations) was due to its pluralism, to the fact that no single institution or value had succeeded in imposing itself to the exclusion of others. Thus, European civilization had involved prolonged competition between theocratic, monarchical, aristocratic and democratic claims. None had succeeded in claiming a monopoly of authority or imposing itself completely on the human conscience—thus, the so-called moral law competed with *raison d'état*, the claims of birth and wealth with those of numbers, the austerity of a life governed by other-worldly values with a life devoted to accumulation, prudential calculation with the love of display or a contemplative life. The question which Guizot's lectures must have raised with his audience—and not least in the young Tocqueville's mind—was how this pluralism of European civilization could survive the destruction of a corporate society, the collapse of different social orders into a 'middle class' condition. Would a new bourgeois ethic achieve the complete ascendancy which had previously been denied any one claim? If so, the danger facing the democratic West was not an anarchy of opinion, but insufficient competition between opinions, a kind of moral stagnation. The new danger was that the postulate of moral equality which was a legacy of Christianity and which underlay the democratic social revolution might give rise to a false and dangerous conclusion—the conclusion that opinions were right simply because they were widespread. The imagination of democratic man was vulnerable to this kind of democratic heresy, in which the liberty implied by moral equality was abandoned in favour of conformity.

What had misled the aristocratic party in France was the subversive associations 'reason' had acquired in the struggle against social privilege under the *ancien régime*. In America, Tocqueville noticed, the right of private judgement did not have the nihilist or anti-religious quality it had acquired in eighteenth-century France, when championed by the *philosophes*. The cause was that, whereas incredulity had become a weapon in the attack on social privilege in France, in the United States the right of private judgement coexisted with universal acceptance of the Christian moral beliefs which had presided over the birth of society. Consequently, the reign of religion itself was there guaranteed by public opinion. 'If we examine it very closely, it will be perceived that religion itself holds sway there much less as a doctrine of revelation than as a commonly received opinion' (*OC* Ib. 18).

Even the prevailing conception of God and his relation to mankind reflects social conditions. Aristocratic man's imagination runs most readily to polytheism, while democratic man's imagination inclines towards monotheism. Social conditions in each case leave their mark.

Men who are similar and equal in the world readily conceive of the idea of one God, governing everyone by the same laws and granting to everyone future happiness on the same conditions. The idea of the unity of mankind constantly leads them back to the idea of the unity of the Creator; while on the contrary in a state of society where men are broken up into very unequal ranks, they are apt to devise as many deities as there are nations, castes, classes or families, and to trace a thousand private roads to heaven. (*OC* Ib. 30)

The Christian Church reflected these pressures during the Middle Ages. Clinging to its belief in one God, it none the less 'multiplied and unduly enhanced the importance of his agents', Tocqueville notices. 'The homage due to saints and angels became an almost idolatrous worship for most Christians, and it might be feared for a moment that the religion of Christ would regress towards the superstitions which it had overcome' (*OC* Ib. 31). By contrast, once the social barriers between men have been lowered, their minds move almost irresistibly towards the idea of a single deity who treats all humans alike.

The most basic habits of mind, then, are influenced by aristocratic and democratic social conditions. When society is divided into permanent ranks or classes, men are more adept at noticing differences than similarities. 'Only one of these classes is ever in view at the same instant; and, losing sight of that general tie which binds them all within the vast bosom of mankind, the observation invariably rests, not on man, but on certain men.' The imagination of aristocratic man is shaped accordingly. 'Those who live in this aristocratic state of society never, therefore, conceive very general ideas respecting themselves; and that is enough to imbue them with a habitual distrust of such ideas and an instinctive aversion for them' (*OC* Ib. 21–2). The opposite habit prevails under democratic social conditions. When men are similarly circumstanced and increasingly resemble each other, the mind cannot consider one sector of society without embracing the whole. Truths that apply to one, appear to apply equally to all, and when men have developed the habit of generalizing in their everyday concerns, they naturally carry that habit over into all their other pursuits. Not surprisingly, the search for laws which unify discrete events becomes the dominant intellectual passion of democratic societies. It shapes the understanding of both nature and culture. The human mind becomes less descriptive and more analytical. Prose is less vivid and singular, more impersonal and neutral.

Such habits of mind also create different approaches to understanding the human past. Those who write history in aristocratic society are accustomed to contemplating a relatively small number of actors dominating the scene. For them, public life is the preserve of a privileged class. 'Historians who write in aristocratic ages are inclined to refer all occurrences to the particular will and character of certain individuals; and they are willing to attribute the most important revolutions to slight accidents.' Yet historians who write in democratic ages have exactly the opposite inclination. 'Most of them attribute hardly any influence to the individual over the destiny of the race, or to citizens over the fate of a people; but, on the other hand, they assign great general causes to all petty incidents' (*OC* Ib. 89). The weakness of aristocratic history is that it tends to overlook general causes and gives undue importance to human intentions. But the danger attached to historical writing in a democratic age is just the opposite, for then historians are enamoured of general systems, which often obscure the role of free will and deny that people have the power of modifying their own condition, subjecting them 'either to an inflexible Providence or to some blind necessity'. At worst, such systems can undermine the will of peoples to modify their own condition and lead them into historical fatalism. 'If this doctrine of necessity, which is so attractive to those who write history in democratic ages, passes from authors to their readers till it infects the whole mass of the community and gets possession of the public mind, it will soon paralyse the activity of modern societies and reduce Christians to the level of the Turks' (*OC* Ib. 92).

Tocqueville's attack on doctrines of historical necessity reveals that his exploration of the meaning of action in two types of society is far from being merely speculative. A new form of self-knowledge—an understanding of how our feelings, ideas, and habits are influenced by the type of society we live in—can, in principle, make it possible to correct the biases which are undesirable consequences of a particular condition of society. That possibility of using a new form of knowledge to offset certain tendencies of a democratic society provided the theme of the final section of the 1840 *Democracy in America*. Here Tocqueville relates the political arguments of the 1835 book to his new sociological explorations.

Tocqueville identifies what he calls 'individualism' as the chief weakness of a democratic social structure. The idea had its roots in the Great Debate. For if the dangers of 'centralization' had provided the theme of the 1835 *Democracy in America*, the notion of 'atomization' *(la société en poussière)* dominates the later book. Individualism is a development of the Restoration liberals' idea of atomization, but, just as in the case of centralization, Tocqueville significantly revises the original use of the idea. It is important to understand what Tocqueville calls individualism. For he carefully distinguishes it from 'selfishness' or an exaggerated love of oneself. Individualism is an attitude generated by a particular structure of society,

a mature and calm feeling, which disposes each member of the community to sever himself from the mass of his fellows and to draw apart with his family and his friends, so that after he has thus formed a little circle of his own, he willingly leaves society at large to itself . . . Selfishness blights the germ of all virtue; individualism, at first, only saps the virtues of public life; but in the long run it attacks and destroys all others and is at length absorbed in downright selfishness. Selfishness is a vice as old as the world, which does not belong to one form of society more than to another; individualism is of democratic origin, and it threatens to develop in the same ratio as equality of conditions.   (*OC* Ib. 105)

Individualism amounts to a withdrawal from the public domain, from a larger involvement in and responsibility for the welfare of society. It stands opposed to what an older republican tradition had called civic virtue or public spirit. It represents an exaggerated and dangerous privatizing of life.

To what extent is individualism inseparable from democratic societies? Certainly it is always latent, for a democratic society dissolves the involuntary associations which had constituted an aristocratic society and puts everyone on the same level, formally equal and free. That formal separation of individuals makes it necessary for everyone to identify and pursue his own interests. Pursuing one's own interest is in that sense 'imposed' by social equality: it is the inner, moral dimension of a civil society.

In an aristocratic society the moral world is utterly different. For the permanent associations of such a society mean that a person's identity is inseparable from that of others *of his kind*. Men feel tied to their ancestors and their descendants, so that 'all generations become . . . contemporaneous'. A powerful bond results. 'A man almost always knows his forefathers and respects them; he thinks he can already see his remote descendants and loves them.' Hence aristocratic man 'willingly imposes duties on himself towards the former and the latter, and will frequently sacrifice his personal gratifications to those who went before and those who will come after him' (*OC* Ib. 105). The fact that a man identifies not with society at large, but only with one class or corporation in it, intensifies his loyalties. That is why the lowering of social barriers and spread of the idea of human equality, while extending the range of human sympathy, diminishes its intensity. Selfless service to others becomes rarer. In aristocratic ages 'the notion of human fellowship is faint and men seldom think of sacrificing themselves for mankind; but they sacrifice themselves for other men'.

The competitive situation in which a democratic society places its members obliges them to pursue their private interests. Indeed, Tocqueville's argument suggests that the very idea of a private sphere is a consequence of civil equality. With the new mobility of property, the number of people who are neither rich nor poor steadily increases, and in this new middling social condition people feel 'they owe nothing to any man and, so to speak, expect nothing from any man; they acquire the habit of always considering themselves as standing alone, and they are apt to imagine that their whole destiny is in their own hands'. It is that impression which can stimulate the growth of individualism. 'Not only does democracy make every man forget his ancestors, but it hides his descendants and separates him from his contemporaries; it throws him back constantly upon himself alone and threatens in the end to confine him entirely within the solitude of his own heart' (*OC* Ib. 106). In its extreme form individualism becomes mere egotism.

Yet the growth of individualism is not inevitable. The moral isolation of men from one another is chiefly a threat when a society has become democratic by destroying aristocratic privilege. Then the struggles of the transition survive as feelings of resentment and contempt among those formerly privileged, feelings of triumph and anxiety among those formerly disadvantaged. 'It is, then, commonly at the outset of democratic society that citizens are most disposed to isolate themselves,' Tocqueville emphasizes. 'Democracy leads men not to draw near to their fellow creatures; but democratic revolutions lead them to shun each other and perpetuate in a state of equality the animosities that the state of inequality created' (*OC* Ib. 108). Tocqueville here returns to the theme of the distortions accompanying the transition from aristocracy to democracy. In the 1835 *Democracy in America* the major distortion examined was an over-centralized or bureaucratic form of the state; in the 1840 *Democracy in America* he examines its moral and social counterpart, individualism.

Individualism is always latent in a democratic society because civil equality, which can be viewed from the angle of the individual rights it creates, from another angle can be seen as requiring decisions and actions which serve private goals, a competitive frame of mind. But when individualism ceases to be merely latent and people withdraw from public affairs in favour of private pursuits, a fatal alliance between individualism and centralization can develop. A bureaucratic form of the state then exploits the formal separation of men in a democratic society and turns it into a real dissociation.

Despotism, which thrives on fear, sees in the isolation of men the best guarantee of its own survival, and therefore it takes enormous care to isolate them ... Equality places men side by side, unconnected by a common tie. Despotism raises barriers to keep them apart: the former predisposes them not to consider their fellow creatures, the latter makes general indifference a sort of public virtue. (*OC* Ib. 109)

Royer-Collard had argued in the 1820s that an 'atomized society' gives rise, inevitably, to centralization. But Tocqueville has now refined the concept of atomization—distinguishing the formal separation of individuals intrinsic to a democratic society, from their real dissociation, which is a withering of the habit of association and of public spirit. Bureaucratic despotism emerges as a perpetual threat to democratic societies because it thrives on the moral attributes which they can so easily foster—a privatizing of concerns and indifference to the fate of others. But it is *not* inevitable.

Here again American institutions proved instructive. 'The Americans have combated by free institutions the tendency of equality to keep men asunder, and they have overcome it' (*OC* Ib. 110). Local autonomy or self-government obliges citizens to come together, to discuss their common needs. In doing so it draws them out of a preoccupation with private interests, and makes them aware of the interests of others. It helps them to understand how the formal independence which civil equality grants does not prevent them from being really dependent upon others. 'As soon as a man begins to deal with common affairs in public, he perceives that he is not so independent of his fellow men as he had at first imagined, and that in order to obtain their support he must often lend them his co-operation (*OC* Ib. 109). Tocqueville anticipates a paradox which governed the later French sociologist Durkheim's work—the paradox that as a market economy and the division of labour develop, the sense of personal independence grows, whereas in a more primitive or subsistence economy, where men do in fact depend less on co-operation, they have a stronger sense of dependence on others.

Representative institutions at the centre of a nation are not by themselves an adequate guarantee against individualism. Local and regional institutions, which can serve as 'schools of citizenship', are necessary to subdue individualism.

The legislators of America did not suppose that a general representation of the whole nation would suffice to ward off a disorder at once so natural to the frame of democratic society and so fatal; they also thought that it was desirable to give political life to each portion of the territory in order to multiply indefinitely the opportunities of acting in concert for all members of the community and to make them feel their mutual dependence. (*OC* Ib. 110)

Thus, the opportunity to participate in public affairs has a crucial moralizing potential. It leads people to ask what serves the public weal rather than merely their own interest. It enlarges their views and prepares them to make sacrifices for the sake of others. Those attributes, in turn, make coercion or state power less important as the source of public order.

Local autonomy generates a habit which is at the heart of free *mœurs*, the habit of association. Without that habit, the members of a democratic society are powerless. They are equal, but equally weak. That makes associations indispensable in a democratic society. They provide a substitute for aristocratic powers.

Aristocratic communities always contain, amidst a multitude of people who are by themselves powerless, a small number of powerful and wealthy citizens, each of whom can achieve great undertakings single-handed. In aristocratic societies men do not need to combine in order to take action, because they are strongly held together. Every wealthy and powerful citizen constitutes the head of a permanent and compulsory association, composed of all those who are dependent upon him . . .

Among democratic nations, on the other hand all citizens are independent and weak; they can hardly do anything by themselves and no one can oblige his fellow men to lend him their assistance. They all, therefore, become powerless if they do not learn to help one another voluntarily. (*OC* Ib. 114)

Americans formed associations for every imaginable purpose—not just commercial, but every other kind, serious and frivolous, moral and aesthetic. These associations served to identify needs and suggest means of action to people who would otherwise be isolated from one another.

When a democratic society has developed free *mœurs*, with local autonomy and the habit of association, it tends to turn individuals into citizens. Free institutions lead, often insensibly, from the pursuit of narrow self-interest to what Tocqueville calls the principle of self-interest 'rightly understood'. That principle does not call for heroic sacrifices or the loftiest forms of self-abnegation, calls characteristic of societies where a leisured, privileged class shapes moral ideas and rhetoric. In a society where everyone is on the same level, and all are thrown into the market-place, it would be futile and even absurd to expect people to disregard their own interests. They have no choice but to pursue their own advantage. But political participation and the habit of association lead people to learn to combine their own advantage with that of others. They learn to identify their own interest in a new way, so that 'an enlightened regard for themselves constantly prompts them to assist one another and inclines them willingly to sacrifice a part of their time and prosperity to the public welfare' (*OC* Ib. 128).

The principle of self-interest rightly understood establishes a balance between private and public interest, by showing how concern for the interests of others in the long run serves one's own interest. 'The principle of self-interest rightly understood produces no great acts of self-sacrifice, but it suggests daily small acts of self-denial' (*OC* Ib. 129). It fosters foresight, moderation and benevolence. Altogether, the principle of self-interest rightly

91

understood is the formal expression of the attitudes and habits associated with free *mœurs*.

These qualities combat the potential weakness of a democratic society. When dissociation is the threat, the antidote must be association. 'If men are to remain civilized or to become so, the art of associating together must develop and improve in the same ratio to which the equality of conditions is increased' (*OC* Ib. 117). For if that art is not mastered, democratic societies will succumb to bureaucratic tyranny, which thrives on the isolation of people from one another and perpetuates it. Once the involuntary associations of an aristocratic society disappear, only two alternatives remain—flourishing voluntary associations or dangerously exaggerated state power.

In at least two major respects, Tocqueville anticipated political developments of the twentieth century, yet, somewhat unhelpfully, he described both as 'democratic despotism'. It is important to distinguish them. One was a bureaucratic despotism founded on fear and justified in the name of a party or leader claiming to defend the popular will against 'enemies' of the people. It was especially this kind of democratic despotism, foreshadowed by Bonaparte's Empire, that Tocqueville had in mind when writing the 1835 *Democracy*— a police state based on fear of the restoration of social privilege, whether from within or without. That model of democratic despotism returned to haunt him after 1851, when Napoleon's nephew restored the Empire with the help of a new threat—the spectre of socialism which so alarmed the French peasantry and middle classes.

But in the 1840 *Democracy* Tocqueville had in mind rather a different kind of despotism—a subtler and, perhaps, in the long run, a more dangerous kind. It was a democratic despotism which would not resemble earlier forms of despotism because it would, ostensibly, be far more benevolent. The extension of state power would no longer be constrained by a traditional social hierarchy. Moreover, it would be justified in the name of welfare and ward off criticism by citing the high level of social services it provided. Indeed, armed with the slogan of the general interest, its means of control would be presented as social services, a kind of liberation.

Through its bureaucracy this new democratic despotism would

attempt to anticipate and provide for all the needs it deemed legitimate:

I want to imagine under what new traits despotism will appear in the world. I see an innumerable multitude of similar and equal people who turn incessantly in search of petty and vulgar pleasures, with which they fill their soul. Each, standing apart, is like a stranger to the destiny of the others; his children and personal friends forming for him the entire human race. As for the remainder of his fellow citizens, he is beside them, but he does not see them. He touches them, but does not feel them. He exists only in and for himself, and even if he still has a family, one can say that he no longer has a country. Above these people rises an immense and tutelary power, which alone takes charge of assuring their pleasures and looking after their fate. It is absolute, detailed, regular, foresighted, and mild. It would resemble paternal power, if, like it, its object was to prepare men for maturity. But it only seeks, on the contrary, to fix them irrevocably in childhood. It wants the citizens to enjoy themselves, provided that they think only of that. It willingly works for their happiness. But it wants to be the only agent and final arbiter of that happiness. It looks after their security, foresees and assures their needs, facilitates their pleasures, regulates their principal affairs, directs their industry, controls their legacies, divides their bequests. Why does it not entirely remove the trouble of thinking and the difficulty of living? In that way it makes even less useful and rarer the exercise of free will, enclosing the action of the will in an ever smaller space ... Equality has prepared men for all these things. It disposes them to endure them and often even to regard them as a benefit. (*OC* Ib. 324)

Such a democratic despotism would be peculiarly hard to resist.

By 1840 Tocqueville foresaw not only the demand for greater social regulation which erupted in the socialist movement of February 1848, but also the more gradual development of the twentieth-century welfare state. When he came face to face with socialism in 1848, Tocqueville decided that its foremost characteristic was its desire to extend state power.

Take whatever name you like, any name except that of democrats. That I forbid you to take. For you do not deserve it ... Whoever invokes democracy invokes the largest possible amount of liberty accorded to each citizen, rich or poor, powerful or humble ... How then could democracy be an equal servitude? No, it is an equal liberty ... All the bonds which the socialists want to re-establish today, are they not the bonds which the French Revolution destroyed? The State is put in the place of the master and of self-direction. (*OC* IIIc. 193–5)

The socialist attack on private property rights struck him as, above all, a new step in centralization. For property rights, whatever problems they created, had a crucial role in dispersing power.

Tocqueville did not oppose welfare measures as such. But he always looked upon the centralization of power under the guise of paternalism as subverting the development of human character and undermining free will. In the new democratic form of paternalism, 'the will of man is not shattered, but softened, bent, and guided. Men are seldom forced by it to act, but they are constantly restrained from acting'. Creating an idiom which anticipates Nietzsche, Tocqueville concludes that democratic paternalism 'does not tyrannize, but it interferes, enervates, extinguishes, and stupefies a people, until each nation is reduced to nothing better than a flock of timid and industrious animals, of which the government is the shepherd' (*OC* Ib. 324–5). Ultimately, then, the development of human character and the dispersal of power should be seen as causes which stand or fall together.

Yet the fact remains that Tocqueville was no *laissez-faire* liberal. His conception of Christian morality continued to play a part in his doctrine which he seldom acknowledged so frankly as in his contribution to the Assembly's discussion of the 'right to work' in 1848.

The French Revolution had the desire—a desire which not only made it holy, but sacred in the eyes of the people—to introduce charity into politics. It conceived of duties of the State to the poor, towards citizens who suffer, an idea more extended, general and higher than anything previously imagined. It is that idea which we must take up—not, I repeat, by putting the foresight and wisdom of the State in the place of individual foresight and wisdom, but by coming readily and effectively, through the means which the State can dispose, to the help of those who suffer and to the help of those who, having exhausted their own resources, would be reduced to misery if the State did not give them a hand. (*OC* IIIc. 179–80)

Tocqueville never recovered from the religious torment which followed his loss of faith in the 1820s. 'The February Revolution must be Christian and democratic; but it must not be socialist. Those words sum up my entire thought.'

The 1840 *Democracy* reveals just how distinctive Tocqueville's liberalism had become. He negotiated a path between civic virtue and individual freedom, between politics and religion, between a free market and a welfare role for government founded on the claims of Christian charity. But perhaps Tocqueville's greatest talent was that, from an aristocratic background, he had a sharp eye for regimes which founded power on the resentments of a class which had once been oppressed. For he saw how the oppressed can become their own oppressors. The greatest contribution aristocratic pride could make to modern democratic societies was to show how self-respect in a society of equals required self-government. To give over the supervision of one's own welfare to others is the role of a lackey, not a citizen.

5 Religion and Social Structure

Tocqueville's development as a thinker was apparently interrupted from 1840 to 1848, because, after his election to the Chamber of Deputies, he was immersed in politics. Even during the long summer breaks there were always parliamentary reports to write or constituents to visit. He had become active in local as well as national politics, and by the mid-1840s was the leading figure in his Normandy *département*. These new duties devoured Tocqueville's time. So did his attempt to keep abreast of the colonizing of Algeria, the great French overseas enterprise of his day. The failure of French colonization under the *ancien régime* had aroused his curiosity when he visited Canada in 1831. Now he wished to help French policy avoid similar mistakes, mistakes he traced to administrative centralization. This study gave him the chance to travel again. However, when he visited Algeria in 1841, he fell seriously ill. He could no longer take his health for granted.

Yet, despite his new political duties and precarious health, Tocqueville did not stop grappling with speculative questions after 1840. He retained an intellectual's impatience. He found day-to-day parliamentary gossip and manœuvring tedious, and soon began to look for relief in ideas. In 1843 the Academy of Moral and Political Sciences asked him to undertake a study of modern moral doctrines, with a view to establishing what, if anything, was original in them. Had seventeenth- and eighteenth-century philosophy really added anything to the stock of basic moral beliefs in Europe?

With so many demands on his time, Tocqueville decided that he could not carry out the task unaided. As it happened, he had recently met a clever and underemployed, if rather strange young man, Arthur de Gobineau. Tocqueville was attracted by Gobineau's passion for ideas, but he also felt sorry for him. Claiming, somewhat dubiously, an aristocratic background, Gobineau had found no clear role in post-Revolutionary society. His passion for ideas was partly a means of finding an identity for himself in the face of social change. Tocqueville, who had struggled to do the same fifteen years before, must have felt a tug of sympathy when he contemplated his young acquaintance's quandary. So he invited him to become his research assistant.

Gobineau was only in his mid-twenties, yet he had already sampled a number of ways of life. After flirting with poetry and Islam—he at one time wore a turban—Gobineau had been forced to take a job in the post office, which he abandoned in 1840 to establish himself as a *littérateur*. He depended on journalism for his small income. As if to compensate, Gobineau's sympathies were fiercely aristocratic and legitimist. In fact, he came from a bourgeois family of the Gironde, though his maternal grandfather was rumoured to have been a bastard of Louis XV. Perhaps that idea consoled the young Gobineau as he tried to cope with his father's poverty and his mother's flagrant promiscuity (something which even led her to prison for a time).

From the outset Tocqueville had doubts about the direction in which Gobineau's mind might develop. 'You have varied knowledge, much intelligence and manners of the best sort, which one cannot help appreciating however much a democrat one may be', he wrote on 8 August 1843. 'Add to all these things another which will flatter you less, which is that one does not know, in becoming acquainted with you, what will become of all these qualities or whether the widespread maladies of the century by which you are affected as much as your contemporaries will not make them useless' (*OC*, IX. 43). Something put Tocqueville on his guard, and when they began to discuss eighteenth-century moral doctrines, Tocqueville's doubts grew. He found in Gobineau not only a hatred of democracy, but an ill-concealed contempt for Christianity. Gobineau argued that the most important propositions in eighteenth-century moral philosophy had nothing to do with Christianity—indeed, that there was a radical discontinuity between its prescriptions and those of eighteenth-century doctrines such as utilitarianism.

Gobineau's judgements disturbed Tocqueville. They threatened the point of view he had developed, with such effort, after his crisis of faith in the 1820s. Gobineau's attitudes ran counter to the interpretation of European history he had learned from Restoration liberals such as Guizot. A fascinating and impassioned correspondence between the two men followed. At issue was nothing less than the relationship between belief and social structure. Tocqueville had been led by Restoration liberals to see a profound connection between the democratic direction of social change in Europe and Christian moral beliefs. That connection had contributed to his 'conversion' to liberalism and to his belief in the superiority of European civilization. Now it was under threat.

To understand how much was at stake for Tocqueville, it is important to notice why Restoration liberals had come to argue as they did. Because political argument under the Restoration took a more historical and sociological form than in the eighteenth century, it raised, by implication, a question about the sources of social change. Eighteenth-century philosophical materialism had settled the question almost casually, while the Scottish Enlightenment had pointed, in an undoctrinaire way, to the 'mode of subsistence' as the major factor in social change. By the early nineteenth century, however, Catholic critics of the Enlightenment such as Maistre and Bonald put forward a very different answer to the question. They argued that the revolutionary crisis in Europe was due to moral apostasy, a falling away from Catholic doctrine as expounded by the Papacy. In their view, neither true moral authority nor the social hierarchy ordained by God could survive, unless the disintegrating effects of the Protestant-inspired right of private judgement were extirpated.

Restoration liberals who were also Protestants—Madame de Staël, Constant, and Guizot—thus had to fight on two fronts. As Protestants, they rejected the view that liberalism was necessarily the ally of atheism or philosophical materialism, whilst at the same time they rejected the view of Maistre and Bonald that the democratic direction of social change in Europe was the result of a falling away from Catholic doctrine. Instead, they urged their readers to understand the disappearance of ancient slavery and the destruction of feudalism as evidence of the gradual penetration of Christian belief in human equality. Thus, in calling for the establishment of civil equality, liberalism was simply working out the implications of Christian moral beliefs. Guizot had, in effect, claimed that liberalism was applied Christianity.

What Restoration liberals did was to historicize the theory of Natural Law. With their polemical need to establish a narrative link between Christianity and liberalism, they abandoned arguments based on a 'state of nature', and instead, presented the stages of European development as evidence of Christian morality transforming social institutions over the centuries. They claimed that the aristocratic institutions established in Europe after the Germanic invasions were essentially foreign to Christian beliefs but, in the circumstances, unavoidable. European history from the early Middle Ages became the story of the subversion of aristocratic beliefs and practices from within by progressive understanding of Christian norms. Thus, Madame de Staël identified three stages in European development—'aristocratic liberty' (liberty for a few), equal subjection (to an absolute monarch) and, finally, equal liberty and representative government (with the English leading the way).

Protestant liberals helped Tocqueville to take a view of the nature of social order which put a premium on belief rather than material factors or mere force. In *Democracy in America* (1835) Tocqueville had used that conclusion to criticize Montesquieu's account of Oriental Despotism.

Montesquieu, in attributing a peculiar force to despotism, does it an honour which I think it did not deserve. Despotism by itself can maintain nothing durable. When one looks closely, one sees that what made absolute governments long prosperous was religion, not fear. Look where you will, you will never find true power among men except in the free concurrence of their wills. Now, patriotism and religion are the only things which will make the whole body of citizens go persistently forward towards the same goal. (*OC* Ia. 99)

In Tocqueville's view, religious belief plays a crucial role in shaping social structure. But that did not mean that all religions are on the same level. By creating a role for conscience or free choice, Christianity had acquired a potential for social progress that other religions have lacked. In that sense, Christianity could be described as the religion of free men, one which gave European civilization a decisive advantage in the long run. That was the special significance of the Reformation for Protestant liberals such as Madame de Staël, Constant, and Guizot. It may be that Tocqueville's inability to accept Catholic dogma represented a partial conversion to that Protestant viewpoint. There is no doubt that he accepted their view about the desirability of separating Church from state.

It is hardly surprising therefore that Tocqueville found Gobineau's views so disturbing as their correspondence developed in 1843. Tocqueville opened the argument by doubting whether modern moralists—by which he meant philosophers since the seventeenth century—had really introduced a new foundation for the rights and duties of man. Rather, they had drawn out new implications from moral premisses laid down by Christianity. He identified three such premisses. First, Christianity had turned an earlier ranking of virtues upside down, placing the 'half-savage' virtues of strength and pride at the bottom of the list, while raising the gentle qualities of sympathy, pity, and humility to the top. Secondly, it extended the sphere of moral obligation from a privileged citizen class to the whole of mankind, thus affirming the equality and the unity of the human race. Thirdly, Christianity removed the sanction of morality from this world to the next, and in that way spiritualized the motives of action.

It is true, of course, that modern moral philosophers have drawn new consequences from these Christian principles because 'our religious beliefs have become less firm and the view of the other world more obscure' (*OC* IX. 46). In democratic societies, where equality is not just a matter for the next world but for this, morality has had to show itself more sympathetic to material needs and pleasures. It also has had to find in this life an additional sanction for moral laws 'which could no longer with security be placed entirely in the afterlife' (*OC* IX. 116). But the underlying moral principles remain those introduced by Christianity. 'Our society has turned away rather from theology than from Christian philosophy', Tocqueville insisted.

Two widespread ideas about government reveal how modern moral philosophy has 'developed or extended the consequences of Christian morality without changing its principles' (*OC* IX. 46). The first is the belief that all men should have equal basic rights, an equal right to at least some of the goods of this world, and that those who have more of these goods should come to the aid of those who have less. The second is a new conception of social justice, which led to charity being transformed from a private virtue to a public duty, a responsibility of the state. That had been the burden of Tocqueville's *Memoir on Pauperism* (1835). The Christian state assumed responsibility for the well-being of people, for repairing the consequences of some inequalities, and coming to the aid of those who could not help themselves. Thus, while accepting that seventeenth- and eighteenth-century philosophy had drawn new consequences from the Christian belief in human equality, Tocqueville insisted that the underlying moral principle—love all men as your brothers—was unchanged.

Only in one respect had modern morality amended Christian beliefs and moved back towards the notions of antiquity. That, Tocqueville argued, was in its new emphasis on civic duty or citizenship.

Christianity and, in consequence, Christian morality established itself outside of all the political powers and even all nationalities. The greatness of its achievement was to form a human society outside all national societies. The duties of men towards each other as *citizens*, the obligations of the citizen towards his fatherland, public virtues in other words seem to me badly defined and rather neglected in the morality of Christianity. That was the weak side of that admirable morality, just as it was the only really strong side of ancient morality. Although the Christian idea of human fraternity has taken complete possession of the modern mind, none the less the public virtues have in our time regained much ground and I am convinced that the moralists of the last century and our own have been preoccupied with them far more than their predecessors ... The modern world has thus taken up and restored to honour a part of the morality of the ancients and has inserted it in the midst of the notions which compose the morality of Christianity. (*OC* IX. 46–7)

This new emphasis on participation, with roots in the ancient conception of citizenship, was now constrained by a strong distributive principle, a Christian-inspired notion of social justice, establishing a kind of social and political morality 'only very imperfectly known to antiquity and which is a combination of political ideas from antiquity and the moral notions of Christianity'.

It was this understanding of the nature of modern social and political morality which made Tocqueville desperately anxious that the conflict between the Christian Church and liberalism in Europe should be overcome. By obscuring the way Christianity sanctioned the principles of liberty and equality, that conflict made it more difficult to create the free *mœurs* which, in his view, were the best guarantee that democratic societies could become self-governing. In a passage omitted from the 1835 *Democracy in America*, he summed up the understanding of Christian morality which governed his exchanges with Gobineau.

Christianity, even when it commands passive obedience in matters of dogma, is still of all religious doctrines the most favourable to liberty, because it addresses only the hearts and minds of those it wishes to submit. There is no religion which has so disdained the use of force as the religion of Jesus Christ . . . When we say that a Christian nation is enslaved it is by comparison with a Christian people that we judge. If we were to compare it to an infidel people it would strike us as free. Christianity, whatever interpretation is given to it, is also of all religious doctrines the most favourable to equality. It is only the religion of J[esus] C[hrist] which has placed the only greatness of man in the accomplishment of duties which anyone can attain . . . (*Democracy in America*, ed. Nolla, i. 224)

It was because of these shared moral commitments that liberalism could plausibly be understood as a secularized form of Christianity and the modern world, crucially, the child of the Church.

Gobineau saw things very differently, however. His strong anti-Christian inclinations led him to argue that there had been a radical break in eighteenth-century philosophy. Not only theology but Christian morality had been discredited. In his view, Christian morality was rendered 'mediocre' by its insistence that 'whoever did not believe could not be virtuous' (*OC* IX. 50). In effect, he ruled out the possibility that Christian moral norms could survive and operate independently of theological beliefs—the crux of Tocqueville's understanding of the course of European history. At first Gobineau probably did not realize that Tocqueville's views were not new or tentative, but had shaped his adult life.

Gobineau's disdain for Christianity affected his account of its origins as well as its moral content. He came close to reducing its origins to the self-interest of the lower classes of antiquity.

They had known the worst side of the right of force, and were happy to defend themselves against violence and by proclaiming the obligations of love and pity. How could obscure artisans groaning every day under the misery which surrounded them, by the misfortunes of all sorts which afflict the poor, possibly resist the desire to chain the arm of the strongest?

The simplest politics would have made it a rule for them to win over populations by promulgating rules which favoured them. (*OC* IX. 49)

It was that instinct rather than any 'reflective or reasoned conviction of what ought to be' which had inspired Christian morality. At the same time (and somewhat inconsistently) Gobineau held that the radical vice of Christian morality was that it subordinated morality to faith, the interests of this world to that of another world. The lack of concern for this world emerged, he argued, in the Christian maxim that suffering is holy, a deadly enemy of social improvement. 'Thus, I think that one can say without injustice that Christian morality is limited to not doing evil, and scarcely goes beyond that limit' (*OC* IX. 50).

The new morality which had appeared in eighteenth-century Europe was not as yet a coherent doctrine, Gobineau admitted. 'It is rather an incoherent collection of consequences drawn from principles which are still for the most part badly defined' (*OC* IX. 49). What clearly distinguished it, however, was a willingness to accept that moral practices did not depend upon religious beliefs. 'The first act [of eighteenth-century moralists] was to detach the chain of relations which bind men to one another from the fashion in which any religious believer conceives of the relations between man and God' (*OC* IX. 51). That step removed any pretext for civil magistrates to interfere with religious belief, and helped to establish religious liberty.

But, according to Gobineau, the eighteenth century took another step. Instead of occupying itself with individual souls in the traditional Christian manner, it sought to identify the causes of poverty and held up the welfare of the largest number, or social utility, as the proper object of legislation. Thus, the maximizing of welfare increasingly replaced the encouragement of individual acts of charity as a goal.

I shall no longer take pity on the unfortunate in order to give him some temporary relief: instead I shall . . . put the government in a condition to destroy misery and to turn every man into a worker serving in the interest of social utility, a worker who ought not to remain inactive. . . . *Everyone has an equal right to work.* Isn't that a very new and different maxim from that of Christ, who said like Moses: *man is condemned to work.* (*OC* IX. 52)

Eighteenth-century philosophy had undertaken nothing less than rehabilitation of the flesh—the substitution of wealth, knowledge, and happiness for the self-sacrifice traditionally enjoined by Christian morality. For Gobineau, such a move away from the resignation and other-worldliness of Christian morality was an undoubted progress in moral ideas, and brought out the close relationship between work and virtue. Because Christianity's plebeian origins perpetually disposed it against any form of self-assertion, it suffered from an irredeemable passivity. 'Its great concern was salvation, and salvation was nowhere so sure as in a profound retreat [from the world], where without temptations and without social duties, there was little opportunity to be useful to other men' (*OC* IX. 50).

For Tocqueville, Gobineau's views absurdly underestimated the moral import of Christianity. 'I must admit that I hold an opinion absolutely contrary to yours about Christianity', he wrote on 2 October 1843. 'It is in my opinion much more different from that which preceded it than you say—I am not a believer (something I am far from boasting of) but unbeliever that I am, I have never been able to repress a deep emotion when reading the Gospels' (*OC* IX. 57). Christianity should not be judged by practices and beliefs inseparable from the barbarous social conditions the Church had to contend with for more than a millennium. Nor should Christian moral beliefs be dismissed because they were bound up with what was not just a morality but a religion—with the emphasis on faith inherent in any religion. The moral crux of Christianity, Tocqueville insisted, was a simple maxim: 'love God with all your heart and your neighbour as yourself. That sums up the law and the prophets' (*OC* IX. 58). Gobineau's assertion that for Christianity 'being good or benevolent towards one's fellows was a duty far less important than believing' was a travesty of that maxim (*OC* IX. 50).

Altogether, Gobineau presented Christianity as a conspiracy of the weak against the strong, the poor against the rich. In a proto-Nietzschean way he turned not merely against the clergy or the Church as an institution, but against the principles of Christian morality. Tocqueville was familiar enough with eighteenth-century anti-clericalism, but he was always inclined to understand it as a rejection of the wealth, immunities, and privileges the Church had acquired through its involvement in an aristocratic society. He found it almost inconceivable that any European could reject the principles of Christian morality, which seemed to him not only elevated, but 'true' or conforming to 'nature'. Where Gobineau found the Koran in many ways superior to the Christian Gospels, Tocqueville argued that from a moral standpoint the Gospels, with their injunction to love all men as your brothers, were purer and less an instrument for control of followers than the Koran. Instead of the moral transparency or purity of intentions which the Gospels sought to introduce into the world, the Koran substituted detailed commands and prohibitions. It sanctioned, in particular, the use of force. That was decisive for Tocqueville—it was a return to the more primitive ideas of the Old Testament.

As their exchanges proceeded, Tocqueville's dismay and disquiet grew. The extent to which Gobineau denied any connection between the democratic direction of social change in the West and Christian moral premisses appalled him. Gobineau was emerging, intellectually, as his *alter ego*. Gobineau's peculiar blend of philosophical materialism, utilitarianism, and élitism was an inversion of all he had come to believe. Though quite unpersuaded by Gobineau's arguments, Tocqueville was almost frightened. It was as if his world were shaking once again, with the moral premisses of his theory of social change being rejected so intransigently.

Little more than a year after they had begun work together, Tocqueville put an end to their research, since Gobineau's hostility to his own conceptions made it unlikely that they could develop any shared interpretation of modern moral doctrines. As Sainte-Beuve had once noticed, Tocqueville remained too much a believer to be able to deepen his understanding of the things which mattered to him most, in the face of such unremitting intellectual hostility. He preferred to pursue his own reflections. Yet his relations with Gobineau did not come to an end. When he became Foreign Minister in 1849, Tocqueville offered Gobineau the chance of acting as his private secretary. He still sympathized with the young man's passion for ideas, despite the unorthodox paths he followed, and this secretarial role would not, moreover, raise the philosophical issues which separated them so profoundly. When

Tocqueville's brief spell at the Foreign Ministry was over, he also managed to secure a post for his protégé in the diplomatic service, which eventually led Gobineau to Persia.

If Tocqueville's disagreement with Gobineau had turned on the continuing role of Christianity in shaping Western moral beliefs, Tocqueville's argument suggested that even the most ostensibly secular modern moral doctrines, such as utilitarianism, had been profoundly influenced by Christian beliefs. It would hardly be too much to say that he held that the Western conception of the individual derived, ultimately, from Christian belief in the equality of men and the unity of the human race, a belief which has served as the foundation for so much ostensibly post-Christian social thought.

The extent to which individuals are not natural facts but cultural artefacts again impressed Tocqueville when he became interested in a subject which allowed him to perform a kind of thought experiment on the relationship between religious belief and social structure. In the mid-1840s, he became interested in India and, especially, in Britain's Indian Empire. His interest was not, at least initially, detached. He foresaw the possibility of conflict between France and Britain. India was the cornerstone of British world power, and he was fascinated by the way Britain had been able to conquer and continued to rule a vast subcontinent. Yet the unintended consequence of Tocqueville's reading about India was a growing interest in the relationship between Hindu beliefs and the Indian caste system. Indeed, he began to wonder if the caste system was anything more than an emanation of Hindu beliefs.

How had Britain been able to conquer and retain India? How could a few thousand Europeans control a subcontinent with a hundred million people? These were questions which, as it seemed to him, Europeans had not yet put to themselves clearly. They were the questions at the forefront of Tocqueville's mind in the mid-1840s when, during summer breaks from Paris, he read British parliamentary reports on India, travellers' accounts and memoirs, as well as earlier histories of India, notably that of James Mill. Great events, such as the British conquest of India, did not just happen. They were not the result of mere chance. It was Tocqueville's firm conviction that 'general causes' lay behind such events, and that they could be identified. When he began, in 1843, to write about India, it was such causes that he wanted to identify. But, in fact, his conclusions did not only clarify the sources of British power in India. They also revealed his conception of the relationship between religious belief and social structure.

In some half-finished chapters on India—for a book he eventually abandoned because he was unable to visit the country—Tocqueville identified several general causes which had paved the way for British conquest. He then proceeded to identify one or two 'circumstances' which had also contributed to that outcome. It was a way of arguing typical of him, for in identifying the long-term or structural elements which shaped events, he tried not to sacrifice short term or 'accidental' causes which also contributed to the outcome. Social analysis should not proceed at the cost of historical over-simplifications.

The first general feature of the Indian scene which Tocqueville considered was the caste system and its effects on feelings. In India, there was nothing like a concern for society as a whole, nothing like the national feeling or patriotism known in European societies. The result of the caste system was that loyalties had an utterly different focus.

There is a multitude of castes in India, but no nation, or rather each of these castes forms a small nation on its own, with its own attitudes, customs, laws and separate government. It is in the caste that the public spirit of the Hindus takes refuge. The fatherland for them is the caste. Elsewhere it cannot be found, but there it is living . . . All the conquerors have easily overturned the political powers of India, upsetting thrones and overturning kingdoms, but the moment they try to interfere with the caste system, they come up against insurmountable difficulties. (*OC* IIIa. 447)

The caste system was, in turn, an emanation of Hindu beliefs, which established radical social inequality at birth. 'The immense majority of Hindus belong to the lower castes', Tocqueville observed. 'Whatever happens, their birth has placed them forever on the last rungs of the social ladder where there is little to hope from government and also little to fear from it—if someone has issued from the feet of Brahma and not from his head, there is nothing to be done' (*OC* IIa. 44).

The second striking thing about Indian history was how little reluctance the natives had shown to being governed by people who did not share their religious beliefs. In that way Indian attitudes contradicted Western expectations about the role of religion. 'A religion which possesses enough empire over souls to have been able to create and maintain a social state so contrary to nature, might be expected to inspire in its believers that sort of fanatical intolerance which takes the place of patriotism in so many barbarous nations' (*OC* IIIa. 448). Yet that was not the case. Brahmanism had always shown itself extraordinarily tolerant and passive in the face of other religions. The reason, Tocqueville concluded, was that Brahmanism was a 'religion of privileges'.

The necessary limits of its believers are those set by race. One belongs to it by right of birth; there is no way of adhering to it when one has not been born into it. For that reason there is no point in conceiving any hatred of those whom Brahma has left outside the pale. It is the idea of the common origin of the human race, the similarity of men and the obligation they all have to know and pray to the same God which has introduced both proselytism and persecution into the world. (*OC* IIIa. 448)

It was a mistake therefore to suppose that all religions were proselytizing by nature.

Tocqueville's reflections on the relationship between Hindu beliefs and the caste system led him to make explicit one of the assumptions underlying his writings. It was an assumption about what makes Christianity distinctive among religions.

When one looks closely, one finds that proselytism, which appears so natural, is only a notion which appears at times and depends upon the prior idea of *the equality of men*. Thus, it is not natural to man. It is Christianity which brought it into the world. And the Mohammedans then borrowed it. Proselytism does not arise simply from the sincerity of belief, but from the idea of the *equality* of men and especially the *unity* of the human race. (*OC* IIIa. 507)

Moral beliefs with universal scope and the proselytizing urge in Christianity were but two sides of the same coin, for no one was excluded categorically from its purview. In Tocqueville's eyes, that was the source of Christianity's dynamic character, while the Hindu religion of privileges accounted for the static or 'petrified' character of Indian society.

The tolerance and passivity of the Hindu religion also had an important political consequence. The Hindus did not react against foreign conquerors on religious grounds. 'The religion which has introduced among them so many vicious institutions and unfortunate maxims, has not therefore produced the only good which might be expected from even the worst religions', Tocqueville observed. For the British were by no means the first non-Hindu rulers of India. Before the British, Persian and Mongol rulers had also been able to establish their rule without provoking any religious reaction or uprising.

The third general feature of Indian society which facilitated British conquest was that local government was merely an aspect of Indian social structure. All important posts in local administration were hereditary. The commune or 'township' (as Tocqueville revealingly described it) was really the fundamental unit of Indian society, and was self-perpetuating, by virtue of the caste system. Thus, revolutions in central government—the rise and fall of dynasties as well as foreign conquest—could take place without compromising or even significantly affecting local administration. For every important local function, whether that of the tax-collector, schoolmaster, preacher, or policeman, was a well-defined role passed on from father to son. Hence 'the commune forms the real social soil of India', Tocqueville concluded. 'Everything above it is agitated, moving and changing. It alone remains firm and stable.'

The task facing would-be conquerors was thus singularly facilitated by the social structure of India. For the only aspect of government which touched the lives of the vast majority of Indians was local government. 'All the political life of the Hindus had retreated into the commune, all the administration was concentrated there.' That fact shaped their political attitudes. 'Provided that the commune subsisted, it mattered little to the inhabitants who acquired the empire—they scarcely noticed the change of masters' (*OC* IIIa. 450). Conquest did not lead to the dissolution of local government as in more centralized European states. Instead, the conquerors simply inherited and manipulated a ready-made instrument, the caste system which carried local government within it.

The three general causes making foreign conquest of India relatively easy were thus: the caste system, which made the mass of Hindus indifferent to who held the reins of central government; a 'religion of privileges' which ruled out proselytism and could not generate a holy war against foreign rulers with different religious beliefs; and, lastly, a system of local administration built into hereditary social roles. To these general or structural features, Tocqueville then added a number of 'circumstances' which had also favoured the British conquest in particular, the fact that the Mogul Empire was in the process of dissolution and no new power had yet supplanted it, and the fact that turmoil following the French Revolution allowed the British to expand in India unchecked by another European power.

On closer inspection, Tocqueville's three general causes *all* prove to be facets of Indian religion. Indifference to 'national' politics, extreme religious tolerance, and stable local administration all derived from beliefs which proclaimed not a universal or human nature, but different natures according to birth or caste. The unequal social identities created and sustained by such a system of beliefs could not generate a dynamic, progressive society. Tocqueville found Hinduism 'extremely enslaving for souls' because it deprived them of responsibility for their own fates, consigning them to limits established by birth. Only in another life, through the notion of reincarnation, could there be any release from existing social roles. Fatalism and the 'petrification' of society were the result. Unlike the Christian West, Indian society had not become self-transforming. 'Once legislation is fixed in a holy writ, it is necessary in the course of time either that belief gives way to civilization or that civilization halts before belief', Tocqueville noted. 'That latter is the case of the Hindus' (*OC* IIIa. 509).

If excessive centralization was the threat to Western societies, in India it was the lack of centralization, either in religious or political authority, which inhibited the development of civilization. Tocqueville's argument implies that the notion of a common or human nature requires some centralization of authority. Without it, both civil and religious society are fractioned into elements which do not recognize any common superior. 'In fact', Tocqueville decided, 'the Brahman religion was composed of a large number of distinct churches.' By the same token, the Brahman religion embraced a large number of often contradictory principles and ideas. 'The result is, I think, that the government of this religion belongs to a caste and not to a hierarchy and that authority is nowhere centralized in it.' Social roles which fail to acknowledge any shared or human nature rule out the possibility of moral bonds between castes. 'The castes exist, but the subordination and relations between castes do not really exist. They are like different nations coexisting on the same soil.'

In such a fragmented society, the worst of all fates is not to belong to one of its many subdivisions, for that is, literally, to be without identity. 'It is important to distinguish the people of low castes from those who have been driven from their castes', Tocqueville notes. 'It is truly the latter whose isolation is complete.' Such people have no acknowledged social role or description. They exist neither as members of a caste nor as individuals in the western sense. They are, in the strictest sense, anomalous.

Tocqueville's discussion of India reveals how he was fascinated by the way religious belief and social structure might deprive humans of the liberty which he believed to be theirs rightfully or 'by nature'. It was that interest in the nature and role of religious belief which separated him from his famous contemporary and friend, John Stuart Mill. A comparison with Mill throws light on the extent to which Tocqueville's devout upbringing by the Abbé Lesueur had left a permanent mark on his mind and shaped his approach to social theory. Mill, by contrast, had been educated in a secular, utilitarian framework by his father, a disciple of Bentham. Mill grew out of this framework of ideas in the 1830s, not least because of his encounter with Tocqueville. Tocqueville's passionate concern for civic virtue as well as his analysis of the strengths and weaknesses of a democratic society aroused Mill's enthusiasm and helped alert him to the limitations of eighteenth-century hedonistic utilitarianism. But 'science' or verification remained Mill's point of reference. The creative role of belief—the sense in which it helps to constitute and sustain different social orders—had an insecure place in Mill's philosophy.

The favourable connotations of 'belief' in Tocqueville's mind created a permanent difference between his outlook and Mill's. It created not so much disagreement as an inability of either to enter fully into the other's mind. When Mill sent Tocqueville a copy of his *System of Logic* in 1843 Tocqueville replied very politely, but his letter implied that Mill's ambitious project for an inductivist 'social science' was not really his sort of thing. Tocqueville contented himself with approving Mill's distinction between necessity and causation as it applied to social explanation. In so doing, he found what common ground he could between them. But the way in which Mill—out of the utilitarian tradition—took 'the individual' as a brute fact was foreign to Tocqueville, who was struck by the radical implications for personal identity of different beliefs and the social structures they helped to maintain. If Mill's approach was rooted in eighteenth-century empiricist philosophy, and its preoccupation with science, Tocqueville was more truly a child of the early nineteenth-century romantic movement in philosophy, with its emphasis on the creative role of belief.

6 *The Ancien Régime and the Revolution* (1856) and full circle

After serving as Foreign Minister in 1849, Tocqueville had no illusions about Louis Napoleon's wish to restore the Empire. The likelihood that Louis Napoleon would succeed put Tocqueville in a quandary, however. For both his political beliefs and his way of life were at stake. He had tied his ambition to the cause of free institutions in France. If Louis Napoleon put an end to parliamentary government there could be no public role for him.

Yet the prospect of inactivity alarmed him. Tocqueville was used to the agitation of public life. He had come to rely upon its excitement to keep his own restlessness at bay. He could not fall back on private life to take up the slack. His marriage was childless, and, while he enjoyed the solitude of the château de Tocqueville after a parliamentary session, he knew himself well enough to realize that after an interval he would need some occupation—an absorbing one, at that—if he was not to fall victim to bouts of depression which had plagued him since adolescence.

How was he to counter that threat? In Sorrento, during the winter of 1850–1, Tocqueville had not only written a memoir of the 1848 Revolution (the *Souvenirs*), but had begun to plan a new book. The subject, as he described it to friends, was to be the emergence of the First Empire—the way the 1789 Revolution, made in the name of liberty, culminated ten years later in a military dictatorship. Such a subject would allow him to comment on the similar transition in France after February 1848, leading to the coup which he expected at any time. He would try to show how, in both cases, class conflict prepared the way for tyranny and administrative centralization provided the means. Tocqueville intended to write analytical or 'philosophical' history, not narrative history. It was the genre he had learned from Guizot in the 1820s. He had neither the wish nor, indeed, the skills needed to write a narrative history of the Revolution.

Yet when he began work in earnest after Louis Napoleon's *coup d'état* in December 1851, the original definition of his subject gave way to another. Instead of writing about the First Empire and the circumstances which gave rise to it, Tocqueville's mind moved back in time. Convinced that Napoleon I's rebuilding of the French state involved a return to the centralizing beliefs and practices of the *ancien régime*, Tocqueville decided that the outcome of the 1789 Revolution could only be understood if its origins were made clear. The *ancien régime* provided the key.

The focus of the book thus shifted. Several chapters which he had already written, dealing with France after Thermidor, Tocqueville was obliged to put aside for later use. However, the shift backwards offered him an enormous advantage. It enabled him to use again the analytical framework he had constructed for his essay, *The Social and Political Condition of France Before the Revolution* (1836). That framework, derived from his reflections on the Great Debate, had led him to argue, in 1836, that despite the survival of feudal jurisdictions, eighteenth-century France was already, in its social structure and form of government, the most modern nation in Europe. Social levelling—especially the subdivision of property—had proceeded further in France, while a bureaucratic form of the state had developed. And the motor of the process had been class conflict.

Tocqueville had never found writing easy. Nor did he from 1852 to 1855. His subject was difficult, but that was not all. The ruin of free institutions under the Second Empire caused him an intense distress. He felt alienated from his age and his nation. He could not bear being reduced for information to the gossip of the Imperial Court or a censored press, after having enjoyed the publicity afforded by parliamentary institutions and a free press.

I cannot tell you how disgust, scorn and weariness are aroused in me by the unproductive, miserable little agitations which still reign here in the remains of the former political class and which, without ever resulting in important acts, produce only a fabric of little intrigues without dignity or meaning. I yearn for my avenue of oaks and the company of my cows. (*OC* VIIIc. 39)

To obtain reliable information, Tocqueville began to subscribe to a German newspaper. He was trying to learn German. The habit of comparison was basic to his mind, and he decided that in order to understand eighteenth-century France he must understand something of eighteenth-century Germany as well.

In that way *The Ancien Régime and the Revolution* came to be set in a wider eighteenth-century European context which had important consequences for the framework of ideas he brought to bear on his subject. The themes of 'atomization' and 'centralization' had been worked out under the Restoration by comparing the development of French and English institutions since the feudal period. They had been designed to reveal why France had developed a despotic monarchy rather than a representative form of government on the English model. Thus, in his 1836 essay Tocqueville had contrasted the way the English aristocracy allied itself with the Commons to limit an over-powerful Crown, while in France a far weaker Crown allied itself with the Third Estate to struggle against the local power of the *noblesse*. The consequence was that the Third Estate acquiesced in the transfer of local liberties to the Crown, until the latter successfully claimed absolute sovereignty. Administrative centralization or the destruction of local autonomy in France was presented as an unintended consequence of conflict between the Third Estate and the *noblesse*.

That analysis of class conflict acts as a premiss for his argument in *The Ancien Régime and the Revolution*. But Tocqueville does not introduce it openly. Instead, it emerges from time to time, as, for example, when he discusses the different connotations of *gentilhomme* and 'gentleman'. The former were symptomatic of a social structure in which prejudices of caste separated the *noblesse* from the bourgeoisie, while the latter was the mark of a society where wealth and education made it possible to enter the governing class or 'natural' aristocracy. The former case was, of course, France, and the latter England.

In *The Ancien Régime and the Revolution*, Tocqueville is concerned less with the origins of French centralization than its effects. Instead of exploring the process by which class conflict had led to centralization in France, he shows how centralization contributed to class conflict by the eighteenth century, keeping classes apart and preventing them from learning to co-operate at the local level. His Appendix on the Languedoc shows that where the effects of centralization were weaker—that is, where self-government survived—class conflicts and caste mentalities were much less intense.

Yet by introducing the conclusions of his 1836 argument,

without the story of class conflict which underlay them, Tocqueville risked making the growth of royal power in France seem almost conspiratorial. Probably in his eyes the advantages outweighed the risk. One advantage was polemical. Writing under the Second Empire, he had no wish to extenuate encroachments by the French state. A second advantage was expository. For the Restoration themes enabled him to identify social levelling and an over-centralized form of government as the crucial features of eighteenth-century France at the very outset of his book.

The postulate of a democratic social revolution provides the substance of Part One of *The Ancien Régime and the Revolution*, while Part Two is dominated by analysis of the nature and consequences of administrative centralization in France. It was in Part Three that Tocqueville found himself writing about topics he had not treated before, especially the role of the *philosophes* and economic trends before the Revolution, and the unsettling effects of political and administrative reforms in the years immediately before 1789.

If Tocqueville's first step in *The Ancien Régime and the Revolution*, as in *Democracy in America*, is to introduce the idea of a revolution in social structure, he now does so less directly. He looks at a number of misinterpretations of the 1789 Revolution, using the idea of a democratic social revolution to explain why contemporaries found it so difficult to judge the nature of the Revolution. At first, other European governments assumed that it was just another political event, which could be exploited to France's disadvantage. Later, when the execution of the King was followed by the Reign of Terror, observers like Joseph de Maistre, instead of minimizing the novelty of events in France, began to interpret them as something demonic and metaphysical, an uprising against moral order itself. Yet both the political and metaphysical interpretations failed to identify the crucial change taking place, the consolidation of a new type of society.

Two other widespread views of the Revolution were mistaken. One was the view that the Revolution sought, chiefly, to destroy the Church and Christianity, while the second was the view that it was directed against political power of any kind—that it was anarchical. In disputing these two views, Tocqueville argues that hostility to the Church would disappear when it ceased to be part of the fabric of feudal privilege. He also argues that social levelling tended to increase, rather than diminish the power of the state, because of the disappearance of intermediate institutions.

Beneath the seemingly anarchic surface there was developing a vast, highly centralized power which attracted to itself . . . all the elements of authority and influence which had hitherto been dispersed among a crowd of lesser, unco-ordinated powers: the three orders of the state, professional bodies, families and individuals. Never since the fall of the Roman Empire had the world seen a government so highly centralized. This new power was created by the Revolution or, rather, grew up almost automatically out of the chaos produced by it.   (*OC* IIa. 85)

The government of Louis XVI was overturned because it was bound up with social privilege. But that was far from a rejection of government *per se*.

What contemporaries failed to understand was that the French Revolution was more the end of a process than its beginning. Long before 1789 the caste society established by feudalism lay in ruins and was being supplanted by another type of society. Even when the forms of feudalism survived they were empty forms by the eighteenth century. The 1789 Revolution merely translated long-standing social and economic facts into the legal and political sphere.

What the Revolution was less than anything else, was a chance event; though it took the world by surprise, it was the only outcome of a long period of gestation, the abrupt and violent conclusion of a process in which ten generations had played an intermittent part. Even if it had not taken place, the old social structure would none the less have been shattered everywhere, here sooner, there later. The only difference would have been that instead of collapsing with such brutal suddenness it would have crumbled bit by bit.   (*OC* IIa. 96)

The 1789 Revolution cut away from French society and government everything associated with feudal or aristocratic privilege.

Feudal institutions had once prevailed everywhere in Western and Central Europe. In the Middle Ages, they formed a kind of social system, as the institutions of France, England, and Germany revealed. 'The community was divided upon the same lines and there was the same hierarchy of classes', Tocqueville emphasized. Just as nobles had the same position everywhere, so town governments were similar and the condition of the peasantry varied only slightly from one place to another. Not only were the institutions of these countries parallel, even the names of practices were often the same—the fief, the manor or *seigneurie*, serfdom, feudal dues and services, trade and craft guilds.

From the fourteenth to the eighteenth century these feudal institutions fell into increasing decay. 'It is no part of my present plan to trace the gradual weakening and decline of this ancient constitution of Europe. I confine myself to pointing out that by the eighteenth century its disintegration had progressed so far that it was half in ruins' (*OC* IIa. 92). Doubtless that decay was more advanced in Western than in Eastern Europe, but its effects were noticeable everywhere. By the eighteenth century social and economic changes—the decline of the feudal nobility, the emergence of intermediate classes, and the new importance of cities and commerce—had turned feudal institutions into a mere veneer. Beneath the veneer, England was already 'quite a modern nation', with equality before the law and the intermingling of classes. On the Continent, and especially in France, a new pattern of government was tied up with social change. 'Central administration was everywhere spreading over the debris of local powers; bureaucratic hierarchy was steadily undermining the power of the nobility' (*OC* IIa. 94).

Tocqueville does not pose directly the question of why social change in Europe had taken a democratic or egalitarian direction, but, just as in *Democracy in America*, he obliquely relates the Revolution to Christian beliefs. First, he insists that 'the Revolution set out to replace feudal institutions with a social and political order, more simple and more uniform, which had the concept of the equality of men as its basis'. Then he denies any incompatibility between Christianity and democracy.

Nothing can be more erroneous than to suppose that democracy is naturally hostile to religion. Neither Christianity nor even Catholicism involves any contradiction to the democratic principle; both are in some respects decidedly favourable to it. (*OC* IIa. 84)

Like Christianity, democratic doctrine asserts the rights and duties of men apart from their membership of any particular society. 'The French Revolution acted, with regard to things of this world, precisely as religious revolutions have acted with regard to things of the other' *(OC* IIa. 89). Both shared a universal moral idiom: both were, by nature, proselytizing.

Tocqueville concludes the first part of *The Ancien Régime and the Revolution* not only by presenting the Revolution more as the end of a process than its beginning, but by insisting that the changes it brought about could just as well have been achieved peacefully by reform. That is the link between the first and second parts of the book, for it raised the question of why a social transformation gradually affecting all parts of Europe led to violent revolution in France. Tocqueville's answer is striking. Revolution broke out in France *not* because France lagged behind, but because it was 'ahead'. The erosion of feudalism had gone further in France. It had not, however, been accompanied by appropriate legal and administrative reforms. Tocqueville placed the blame squarely on centralization. The bureaucratic character of the French state had destroyed local self-government, which brings different social groups into contact with each other, makes them familiar with each other's interests, and teaches them to reconcile those interests.

By the mid-eighteenth century a dangerous discrepancy had developed between the social condition of France and its legal institutions. On the one hand, the principle of formal inequality of rights continued to prevail in public life. Only nobles were allowed to approach the king or carry arms in public, and only nobles could hold great military commands and the conspicuous offices of state. Even more dangerously, the immunities enjoyed by the *noblesse* as a caste included exemption from most forms of taxation, despite the fact that the *noblesse* no longer had responsibility for local government. The *noblesse* had become a mere caste, made conspicuous by privileges which had no clear social utility.

On the other hand, the French were more nearly alike than any other European people. The subdivision of land had long since destroyed serfdom and created a large landowning peasantry, while the wealth of the *noblesse* had steadily declined—in contrast to the wealth of the English aristocracy which had ceased to be exclusive. Indeed, in wealth, education, and habits there was little to distinguish the middle classes in France from the *noblesse*. At the same time administrative centralization had reached an extreme point in France. The Estates-General (the assembly of the three estates: clergy, nobility, and commoners) had been dispensed with, municipal franchises had been put up for sale to increase the Crown's revenue, and village officials had become agents of the state rather than representatives of local people. Provincial and local affairs were almost entirely in the hands of officials appointed by the Crown.

In France, centralization had proceeded much further than elsewhere, and it was that, joined to the fact that so many peasants had become proprietors, which made surviving feudal charges more intolerable in France. Being a proprietor the peasant had become far more commercial in outlook. At the same time, these charges were exacted by local nobles who had lost their role in government and no longer had obligations which justified their privileges. Understandably, that combination of privilege without power enraged the peasantry and provided the seeds for revolution. Thus, paradoxically, feudalism was more hated in France because it scarcely existed any more.

Tocqueville emphasized the way the royal administration relentlessly encroached on other jurisdictions. By ousting the nobles from local and provincial government, the royal administration separated them as a class from the peasants among whom they lived. They lived among the peasants as 'privileged strangers' while the real government of the country was in the hands of *Intendants*, who were mostly from the middle classes. The *Intendants* were chosen by and could only be dismissed by the Controller-General.

Just as the central administration had to all intents and purposes only one executive officer in Paris, so it had only one such representative in each province. It is true that in the eighteenth century we still find great lords bearing the titles of Governors of Provinces. But though they were still treated with deference, they had ceased to have any power. All real authority was vested in the *Intendants*. (*OC* IIa. 109)

The destruction of municipal and provincial autonomy prevented effective local resistance and the royal government was able to raise revenue without regard to social consequences.

In *The Ancien Régime and the Revolution* Tocqueville limited himself to tracing the growth of royal power back to the first introduction of a tax by the Crown which did not require the consent of the Estates General, the *taille.* Increasing resort to that tax over the following centuries, and the wanton destruction of local franchises which the search for new sources of revenue led the Crown into, became the leitmotiv of his analysis of the growth of royal power. In Tocqueville's view, the development of administrative law in France was symptomatic. He saw it as the characteristic instrument of an overcentralized government and as a natural symbol of the centre's ability to evade legal accountability.

It could be argued that, in the absence of the 1836 analysis of class conflict, Tocqueville presented the encroachments of the French state in an over-simple way—as due to the thirst for power of kings and bureaucrats, to the momentum of an administrative machine out of control and fed by delusions of grandeur. In so far as he was not only writing history but attacking Louis Napoleon's Second Empire, such arguments may have suited his purpose. Nevertheless, later historians have criticized Tocqueville for neglecting other causes of French centralization—such as military pressures on a continental state with powerful neighbours, pressures which would apply much less, for example, to England.

Yet the change of focus between the 1836 Essay and *The Ancien Régime and the Revolution* enabled Tocqueville to write the most original and subtle chapters of the book, chapters in which he explored the effects of excessive centralization on different social classes in the last phase of the *ancien régime.* This change of focus enabled him to concentrate on the dissolution of moral ties between the different classes and even within them. He coined a new term to express a new idea, calling such a dissolution of moral ties 'collective individualism'. It was an important variation on the Restoration liberal theme of 'atomization'.

This new idea may have been inspired by the study of Indian castes which he had undertaken in the 1840s. What Tocqueville had found remarkable about Indian society was that different castes had no common loyalties and had no idea of belonging to a larger society or fatherland, social solidarity or sympathy existing only within the various castes. In writing *The Ancien Régime and the Revolution* Tocqueville, whether consciously or not, seems to have turned this Indian model into an ideal type by which he

121

measured the dissolution of social ties in eighteenth-century France. The morally repulsive consequence of administrative centralization in France was that it first made it unnecessary and then made it difficult for social classes to come into contact, destroying their wish to understand one another's needs.

Thus the bonds of practical sympathy between classes steadily narrowed under the *ancien régime*. They ceased to be involved with one another's fate. Of course, the dissolution of social ties stopped short of the Indian caste extreme. The beliefs embodied in Church and State of Christian Europe, especially the belief in a shared or 'human' nature, prevented that. None the less, the fatal flaw of administrative centralization was that it gradually destroyed an earlier 'aristocratic' sense of community while preventing the emergence of a new 'democratic' sense of community. It allowed French society to disintegrate into a congeries of groups, competing for immunities, financial advantages, and status. It nearly destroyed civic spirit in France.

Every class in eighteenth-century France was morally diminished. This was most obviously true of the old *noblesse*. Losing its role in government, its *raison d'être*, proved to be disastrous. Tocqueville remained a harsh critic of the *noblesse*. Their pride took a toll not only of their capacity as a class, but of their wealth too. Failing to notice that 'true' aristocracy entailed leadership, they became mere courtiers fobbed off with baubles and honours by the policies initiated by Richelieu and Louis XIV. The fate of the *noblesse* revealed how false their pride had become.

The French *noblesse* had stubbornly held aloof from the other classes and had succeeded in getting themselves exempted from most of their duties to the community, fondly imagining they could keep their lofty status while evading its obligations ... The more their immunities increased, however, the poorer they became. On the other hand, the middle classes (whom they were so afraid of being merged with) grew steadily richer and more enlightened without their aid, and, in fact, at their expense. Thus, the nobles who had refused to regard the bourgeoisie as allies or even fellow citizens, were forced to envisage them as their rivals, before long as their enemies, and finally as their masters. (*OC* IIa. 189)

The contrast with eighteenth-century England was painful. There, the original feudal class had sacrificed its pride in order to retain a political role and share power with the Commons. A true aristocracy based on wealth and education as well as birth had developed. Local affairs were still controlled by leading local people.

The French bourgeoisie was also a victim of centralization. While acquiescing in the destruction of municipal autonomy the bourgeoisie cut itself off from the peasantry with its own form of pride, a bastard feudal pride. 'Though the nobility and the middle classes followed divergent paths, in one respect they were alike; for the bourgeois ended up by being as isolated from the people as any nobleman', Tocqueville noted sadly. 'Far from showing any concern for the peasants, he shut his eyes to their misfortunes instead of making common cause with them in an attempt to correct social disabilities in which he shared; he deliberately sponsored new forms of injustice which benefited him personally; indeed, he was quite as eager to secure preferential treatment for himself as any noble to retain his privileges.' Thus, the example of the *noblesse* in preferring privileges to power shaped the attitudes and behaviour of the bourgeoisie. For the bourgeoisie, as well as the *noblesse*, the mass of the peasantry had become 'an alien, incomprehensible race of men'. Accepting the tutorship of the state, the bourgeoisie concentrated its efforts on purchasing immunities and becoming state *rentiers*. Attitudes fostered by state tutorship worked against the French bourgeoisie becoming a vigorous commercial class on the English model or developing civic spirit.

If there is a touch of disdain in Tocqueville's treatment of the bourgeoisie, there is no disdain in his account of the peasantry's plight. In his eyes, the peasantry were the chief victims of administrative centralization. What had become a royal habit, if not policy, of separating the classes left the peasantry without leadership. The wealthier, educated sections of society had cut themselves off from the peasantry, leaving it at the mercy of the royal government's unending need for revenue. Immunities from taxation won by the *noblesse* and the bourgeoisie only added to the burden on the peasantry, while the payment of feudal dues humiliated as well as impoverished them.

Living in the countryside as 'privileged strangers', the French *noblesse* deluded themselves into thinking that they were still the people's leaders. 'In reality, however, they led nobody; they were alone, and when an attack was launched on them their sole resource was flight.' The bourgeoisie were in no better position to lead. Torn between hatred of aristocratic privilege—especially when the *noblesse* reasserted their privileges in the decades before 1789—and a wish to join in the ranks of the ennobled, the bourgeoisie never considered making common cause with the peasantry in the interests of civil equality or freer institutions. Just as the nobles lost all concern for the peasants when they gave up their role in local administration, members of the Third Estate who acquired wealth and education abandoned the countryside for the towns. However, accustomed to considering the state machine as their protector, the bourgeoisie came to see local liberties chiefly as a form of property and source of status.

Rather touchingly, Tocqueville was still struggling to understand the moral isolation of his own class in the final decades of the *ancien régime*—the reasons why it suddenly found itself rejected and persecuted. He concluded that the destruction of local autonomy in France had separated social classes so that they were related only by their jealousies and hatreds, not through any habits of working together, or pursuing common interests. Little wonder that the peasantry turned their resentments against the fiscal and other privileges of the 'strangers' who continued to live among them, the *noblesse*.

Two other symptoms of the pathology of the French *ancien régime* fascinated Tocqueville. The first was the growth of Paris. The extinction of local and provincial autonomy drew all the reins of power to the capital, while the growth of industry created an urban proletariat which was to be the chief actor—the Revolutionary Crowd—in successive revolutions after 1789. Thus, while administrative centralization made revolution more likely by destroying the moral ties between citizens and classes, the predominance of Paris made revolution increasingly easy to execute. The sudden collapse of the monarchy would hardly have been possible otherwise.

The condition of minds in France by the late eighteenth century was equally conducive to revolution, for the centralization of administration had left its mark on the way the French thought about public affairs. Lack of experience of government contributed to the reign of excessively general ideas, abstract formulas which blinded them 'to the very real obstacles in the way of even the most praiseworthy reforms' (*OC* IIa. 195). That reliance on abstract formulas contributed to the potential for violence, not least state violence, after 1789.

Tocqueville's attitude towards two important groups under the *ancien régime* had changed since his 1836 Essay. He was less inclined to treat the Church as having become merely an instrument of government. No less critical of the higher clergy than before, he now found that the lower clergy were almost alone in trying to defend and improve the lot of the peasantry—struggling against that moral isolation which otherwise cut the peasantry off from other classes in France. But if Tocqueville regards the lower clergy with a gentler eye in *The Ancien Régime and the Revolution*, his view of the *philosophes* is more astringent than in 1836. Having looked carefully at their writings from the angle of government, he is struck by the extent to which they were unconscious centralizers—how their plans for 'rational' reforms took for granted a central agency which could *impose* them. Their programme presupposed concentrated state power.

In a sense, the *philosophes*, with the notable exception of Malesherbes, took over the role which lawyers had played earlier in the *ancien régime* and provided a justification for the administrative centralization which had destroyed free *mœurs* in France. Only in the very last years of the *ancien régime* did a taste for self-government—in the form of a federalist movement—begin to make headway. But it was far too late. The hatred of privilege was by that time an invincible passion in France, one which boded ill for French experiments with self-government after 1789. The message for his readers was clear enough. Louis Napoleon's Second Empire was only the latest manifestation of centralizing beliefs and practices which had roots deep in the *ancien régime*.

During the years when he wrote *The Ancien Régime and the Revolution* Tocqueville's letters seethe with anger at the follies of Louis Napoleon and the pretensions of his court. Tocqueville found the passivity of the French before this 'upstart' unbearable, though he reserved his sharpest remarks for the complicity of the higher clergy in tyranny. Yet Tocqueville did not expect an early end to the Second Empire, recognizing that Louis Napoleon's skill in founding his Empire on fears of socialism among the peasantry and on the ambitions of the army gave him a hold over the country which could not be broken immediately. Only a foolhardy military adventure might do that. In the long run, as fear of socialism subsided, the pride of the French would rebel at the idea of having so little share in their own government. Then habits and ideas fostered by several decades of representative government (1815–48) might come back into play. Before that time, however, there was little hope.

This bleak assessment of the prospects for France did little to raise Tocqueville's spirits. That, in turn, has contributed to a misconception about his political attitudes. Intensely aware of weaknesses in French society—of the way class conflict, through its influence on *mœurs*, made the achievement of stable representative government far more difficult than in Britain—Tocqueville has been presented as a fatalist who did not think France capable of self-government. But that conclusion does not follow. Tocqueville's belief in human liberty entailed that men were free, within limits, to shape their own future. It followed that France could, even if only slowly and painfully, develop the free *mœurs* which would help to reconcile her democratic social condition with representative government. Even his disappointing experience on the Constitutional Commission of 1848 had not shaken that belief.

Tocqueville remained hostile to fatalism in any form. He had an opportunity to make that clear in the mid-1850s when he found himself locked in argument once again with his former protégé, Arthur de Gobineau. In 1855 Gobineau, who now styled himself Comte de Gobineau, published the last volumes of his *Essay on the Inequality of the Human Races*, the book which made him one of the founders of modern racialist ideology. By this time Gobineau had a diplomatic posting in Persia. His earlier penchant for Islam and hatred of democracy had fused with ideas about the superiority of the Aryan race. These ideas had hardened into a system which cast the Aryans as a superior race threatened by intermixing with other races—ranked on a scale of declining ability and virtue. On Gobineau's analysis, physical inheritance was virtually everything, free will almost nothing; his aristocratic longings had finally led him to see democracy as a form of miscegenation.

When he read the letters from Tehran in which Gobineau

elaborated his doctrine, Tocqueville found that his protégé had become a kind of nemesis. It was not that he was surprised by the turn Gobineau's mind had taken. But his horror at the way Gobineau inverted his own deepest beliefs, and his dread of the harm such racialist doctrines might do, led Tocqueville to reply with some of the most compelling letters of the nineteenth century. They were not, to be sure, easy letters to write. For, despite everything, Tocqueville remained fond of Gobineau, and tried to salvage their friendship, while utterly rejecting Gobineau's ideas. The pain which Gobineau's premisses caused him—premisses which made a mockery of free will—was almost physical.

Even before reading the new volumes, Tocqueville warned Gobineau that he was unlikely to welcome their thesis. 'I have never concealed from you that I had a strong prejudice against what seems to be your leading idea which strikes me as belonging, I confess, to that family of materialist theories and to be one of its most dangerous members, since it involves the fatality of constitution applied not only to the individual but to those collections of individuals which are called *races*' (*OC* IX. 199). After he had read the volumes, Tocqueville shifted the comparison, and described Gobineau's doctrine as a form of predestination, though closely allied to materialism. 'In any case, both theories lead to a very great restriction, if not to a complete abolition of human liberty', Tocqueville wrote to Gobineau, 'Well ... I remain convinced of the extreme opposite of these doctrines. I find them very probably false and most certainly pernicious.'

Tocqueville did not deny that the families composing the human race had acquired different aptitudes and tendencies over time from a variety of causes. 'But that these tendencies and aptitudes are invincible is something which has not only never been proven, but in itself is unprovable, for it would be necessary to dispose not only of the past but also the future to do so' (*OC* IX. 202). Tocqueville argued that it is impossible to reconstruct the ways and degrees in which the different human families have mixed. To rely simply on a racial explanation was to exclude categorically many kinds of causes traditionally identified as shaping the course of human history. 'Do you really think that by taking this way to explain the destiny of different peoples you have thrown much light on history or that knowledge of man has gained from turning away from the path followed . . . by so many great minds who have sought the causes of events in the influence of certain men, sentiments, ideas, and beliefs?' (*OC* IX. 203).

The objection to Gobineau's doctrine on grounds of morality was at least as compelling as the objection on grounds of truth. Or, rather, they were inseparable.

What possible interest can there be in persuading miserable people living in barbarism, idleness or slavery, that by virtue of their race there is nothing that can be done to improve their condition, change their *mœurs* or modify their government? Don't you see that from your doctrine derives naturally all the evils which permanent inequality gives birth to: pride, violence, scorn for one's fellows, tyranny and abjection in all its forms? (*OC* IX. 203)

The assumptions which Tocqueville had acquired in the 1820s were again laid bare. Yet his conception of the origin and nature of liberalism—of liberalism as applied Christianity—also made him see the futility of arguing further with Gobineau. 'There is a whole intellectual world between your doctrine and mine.' The sense of justice which had reconciled Tocqueville to the democratic direction of social change was, for Gobineau, simply further evidence of moral degeneration resulting from the mixing of races and consequent adulteration of the 'pure' Aryan race.

Gobineau's political views were just as odious. During the July Monarchy Gobineau had enjoyed describing French 'bourgeois' politics as sordid and corrupt, a symptom of the democratic 'degeneration' which in his new book he traced to miscegenation. Now, in the mid-1850s, he could not conceal his admiration for Louis Napoleon's Empire. The suppression of political liberty and public debate counted for little with him, when compared to the achievement of what he called 'order' and 'authority'.

In Tocqueville's eyes, it was a familiar enough pattern. It was the same lack of concern with political liberty which he had noticed in many devout Christians under the Restoration and which the French episcopacy reproduced under the Second Empire. Unconsciously perhaps, it was one reason why he found it difficult to consider himself an orthodox believer. 'My heart always rises up at the sight of those little gentlemen who pass their time in clubs or dubious places, or greater types who are capable of every baseness as well as all sorts of violence, speaking of *their holy religion*. I am always tempted to shout at them: "Please be pagans with an upright conduct, a proud heart and clean hands rather than Christians of that sort"' (*OC* IX. 278). Altogether, Gobineau's doctrine was the antithesis of the 'good cause' of free institutions which had inspired Tocqueville's life-work. The sacrifice of pride which Tocqueville's residually Christian conscience had demanded as the price of understanding the direction of social change had never been made by Gobineau. Little wonder that Tocqueville was astonished when, in 1856, Gobineau announced that he had become a Catholic—while admitting disarmingly, that in the past 'undoubtedly I've been at one time or another a *philosophe*, Hegelian or atheist' (*OC* IX. 27). Gobineau's doctrine seemed to Tocqueville diametrically opposed to the foundations of Christian thought. 'You know that I cannot reconcile myself to your system in any way; and my mind is so fixed on this point that the very reasons you put forward to make it acceptable to me strengthen my opposition, which remains *latent* only because of my affection for you' (*OC* IX. 265).

How could Gobineau fail to notice that his theory conflicted with both the letter and the spirit of Christianity?

As for the letter, what is clearer in Genesis than the unity of the human race and the descent of all men from the same man? As for the spirit of Christianity, its distinctive trait is to have sought to abolish all the distinctions of race which the Jewish religion had allowed to subsist and to create a single human species, whose members are all deemed to be equally capable of perfecting themselves and resembling one another?

The crux of Christian morality is 'equal liberty', not permanent inequality. Christianity has clearly tended to make all men brothers and equals. Your doctrine makes them at most cousins whose common father is only in heaven; down here there are only victors and vanquished, masters and slaves by fact of birth, and that is so true that your doctrines are approved, cited and commented upon by whom? By the owners of negroes in favour of eternal servitude which is founded on the radical difference of race. (*OC* IX. 277)

Evidently Tocqueville believed that Christianity was in a peculiar sense the religion of free men. He came close to saying that, properly understood, it abolished authoritative religion, through its emphasis on the role of conscience and free will.

The direction Christianity had long given to European *mœurs* established its superiority in Tocqueville's eyes. He had no patience with Gobineau's Islamic leanings. 'At the same time that you are so severe towards that religion which has contributed so much to placing us at the head of the human race, you seem to me to have a decided weakness for Islam' (*OC* IX. 68). For Tocqueville, the emphasis on conscience and choice in Christianity raised it above the rule-bound doctrine of Islam. His study of the *Koran* had long ago persuaded him of that. 'I emerged from that study with the conviction that there had been few religions considered as dangerous for men as that of Mohammed', he admitted. 'It is, in my view, the principal cause of the decadence today so visible in the Muslim world and although less absurd than ancient polytheism, its social and political tendencies being far more dubious, I regard it relative to paganism as a regression rather than a progress' (*OC* IX. 69). Altogether, it was no accident, in Tocqueville's eyes, that free institutions had developed in the Christian West.

He believed that Christianity had been the primary source for the claim of 'equal liberty', and continued to sustain it through its moral beliefs. In contrast to nineteenth-century radical thinkers who held that science was the key to modernity and social progress, he did not suppose that Christianity was about to be superseded in the West.

I know that there are many people who think that will one day happen and who look out of the window each morning with the idea that they will finally see this new sun rise. As for me, I am convinced that they will always look in vain. I would believe rather in the advent of a new religion than in the growing prosperity of our modern societies without any religion. (*OC* IX. 68)

In Tocqueville's view, it is the nature of religious belief to act on mankind by regulating the ordinary actions of life, to create and sustain *mœurs*. That normative role could not be provided by the natural sciences or indeed by the newly fashionable project of a 'science of society'.

In the last years of his life Tocqueville formed a friendship with a clever, devout woman who occupied an extraordinary position in the European Catholic world. Sophie Swetchine was a Russian who, having been converted to Catholicism in her teens in St Petersburg by the Sardinian Ambassador, Joseph de Maistre, moved to Paris after Napoleon's fall. There Madame Swetchine gradually created a salon marked by a speculative interest in religion and tinged with mysticism—attracting some of the most remarkable men of her day. Although she was twenty years older than Tocqueville, he too found her company strangely consoling. When he first met her his wife's moral and physical condition was worrying. Tocqueville may have found in Madame Swetchine a sympathy free of anxiety which Mary could no longer offer him.

With Madame Swetchine Tocqueville's life came full circle. He re-established with this elderly woman the relationship of complete candour and intellectual sympathy he had enjoyed with the Abbé Lesueur as a boy. A competitive element, which never quite disappeared in relations with his closest friends such as Beaumont and Kergolay, and the constraints which jealousy had introduced into his marriage, were wonderfully absent in his relations with Madame Swetchine. Tocqueville opened his heart to her as to no one else during his last years. Consequently the letters he wrote to her—letters which deserve to be better known—give a unique glimpse of this proud but vulnerable man.

A deep interest in religious questions was the bond which united them. Tocqueville's interest was, however, tinged with doubt. He had saved a few beliefs from the wreck of his childhood faith, but beyond them all was uncertainty. And even the beliefs he retained were not free from occasional buffetings of doubt—buffetings which left him now, as in his sixteenth year, feeling that the earth was shaking beneath his feet. With Sophie Swetchine he was able to discuss openly his attempt to put together a few certainties by which to live. Although they did not meet until the early 1850s, within a short time he was confiding in her.

Their correspondence began just before *The Ancien Régime and the Revolution* was published. Tocqueville was trying to resume work on its sequel, but he found that he suffered from bouts of discouragement which he could do nothing about, even though he understood their source. 'The truth is that both great confidence and lack of confidence in oneself stem from the same source, an extreme desire to shine which interferes with the tranquil and moderate opinion one ought to have of oneself' (*OC* XVa. 264).

Once *The 'Ancien Régime' and the Revolution* had appeared, Tocqueville did not conceal his anxiety about its reception. 'How much I should like to be able to say that, fortified by intentions I had when writing it and with a certain inner sense of the value of the work, I wait calmly for the judgement of the crowd!' he wrote to her.

But unfortunately that isn't the case at all. All the notices of the book which reach me cause an excitement which I am ashamed of. I can only recover a bit by confessing it to you. The greatest part of what I hear gives me pleasure. Certainly, until now, the favourable reception exceeds my expectation. But see how badly made my mind is! The pleasure which approval gives me dwindles rapidly and disappears. The least criticism gives me a chagrin which remains a long time. In truth, Madame, you must have inspired great confidence for me to tell you about these miseries. (*OC* XVb. 281)

His great weakness, Tocqueville decided, was an 'incessant restlessness of mind which . . . reduces the value even of something which has been most desired as soon as it has been attained' (*OC* XVb. 285). He had tried to emulate those who could go through life with their eyes fixed on a goal 'beyond life', but he had never succeeded.

The nearest he had come to finding such an other-worldly goal was in his commitment to liberty. For him, that pared-down conception of Christianity was a matter of instinct as well as belief. It overrode even his desire for literary success and fame.

I regard, as I have always done, liberty as the first of all goods; I continue to see it as one of the richest sources of masculine virtues and great actions. There is no tranquillity or well-being which can hold me away from it. I see, on the contrary, most of the people of my time, even the most upright, . . . who seek only to accommodate themselves as well as they can to a master, and, what completely throws my mind into trouble and a kind of disgust, who try to turn this taste for servitude into an ingredient of virtue. (*OC* XVb. 268)

Tocqueville dwelt on that connection in one of his most eloquent letters to Madame Swetchine.

She had urged that greater equality in this world is the clear implication of Christian doctrine. He agreed, but he insisted on a further point. 'I entirely agree with you', he wrote in September 1856, 'that the more equal distribution of goods and rights is the greatest goal which those who govern can propose to themselves.' But equality should be understood as involving political as well as civil rights. 'I only wish that equality in the political sphere could consist in all being equally free and not, as one more often hears these days, in all being equally subject to one master' (*OC* XVb. 291.–2). The latter was an incomplete, mutilated version of equality. It was perhaps the result of a misunderstanding of the Gospel.

It seems to me that there are in morality two distinct parts, each equally important in the eyes of God, but which his ministers in our day preach with a very unequal ardour. One relates to private life; the duties relative to men as fathers, sons, wives or husbands ... The other has to do with public life, the duties which each citizen has towards his country or the human society of which he is a part. Am I wrong to think that the clergy of our time are very preoccupied with the first part of morality, but very little with the second? (*OC* XVb. 292)

Despite the obvious injustices of the *ancien régime*, Tocqueville argued that at least some of the old French *noblesse* had possessed real public spirit. He recalled the advice which his grandmother had given his father as a child. After extolling the private virtues, she had insisted that a man should never forget that he owes his life to his country.

Christian beliefs should not therefore be interpreted as requiring mere acquiescence in whatever power existed.

I know that people have inferred from the text of the Gospel ... that the duty of the Christian in political matters is simply to obey established authority, whatever it may be. Allow me to think that this is rather in the gloss than in the text or that public virtue for the Christian is restricted to that. Of course, there is no doubt that Christianity can exist under all sorts of government; that is one of the characteristic marks of its truth. It has never and will never be tied completely to one form of government or the fate of a particular nation; even more, it can triumph in the midst of the worst governments and can find in the evils which such bad governments impose on men the matter of admirable virtues. But it does not follow, unless I am mistaken, that it must make people insensitive or indifferent to these evils, and that it does not impose on everyone the duty to deliver his fellows from these evils by whatever legitimate ways his conscience identifies. (*OC* XVb. 297)

Neglect of the public sphere was dangerous precisely because Christian beliefs had helped to create it—separating it from a private sphere, where individuals are deemed to have a right, in conscience, to make their own decisions.

However, such a private sphere does not exhaust the duties flowing from the dictum that men ought to love one another as brothers. That dictum implies not just respect for the autonomy of others, but concern for them—charity or benevolence. With the growth of civil equality and the state, such charity or benevolence became, at least in part, a public responsibility, and the proper discharge of that responsibility imposed a moral duty on all. Thus, Tocqueville argued that Christian thought was in an important respect incomplete. It had never bothered to work out the implications of its own moral beliefs which not only required that public authority be founded on consent, but that Christians ought to take seriously their duty as citizens. The right to be consulted seemed to him to carry a moral duty to take part in public debate and decision-making. The free institutions which made that possible completed Christian moral beliefs.

Why had Christianity neglected so vital an area? Tocqueville's argument implies that the eschatological beliefs of the earliest Christian communities, and their passive attitude towards the Roman state, had left a gap in Christian thought about government, which survived even into the nineteenth century. That gap could, unfortunately, always be exploited by tyrannical regimes, such as the Second Empire.

So completely had Madame Swetchine captured Tocqueville's confidence that in February 1857 he described to her the event which more than any other had shaped his life, his loss of religious certainty. As an episode it was momentous because, he admitted, he had an uncommon need for certainty.

The sight of the problem of human existence constantly preoccupies me and constantly overwhelms me. I can neither penetrate into this mystery, nor take my eyes away from it. It excites me and depresses me by turns. (*OC* XVb. 314)

It was not that he believed nothing. 'I believe firmly in another life, since God who is sovereignly just, has given us the idea; in that other life, in the reward for good and evil, since God has permitted us to distinguish them and has given us the liberty to choose.' But beyond those truths, everything seemed to him wrapped in fearful obscurity.

Tocqueville described how, left to his own devices in the Metz prefecture at sixteen, he had devoured the books in the library— 'piling up in my mind all sorts of notions and ideas which ordinarily belong to a different age'.

My life until then had developed in a setting full of faith, which hadn't even allowed doubt to touch my soul. Then doubt entered or rather thrust itself in with unheard-of violence, not merely doubt of this or that, but universal doubt. I experienced suddenly the sensation described by those who have witnessed an earthquake, when the earth was trembling beneath them, the walls around them, the ceiling above their heads the furniture around them, and the whole of nature before their eyes.   (*OC* XVb. 315)

The effect on his feelings had been catastrophic. 'I was seized by the blackest melancholy, disgusted by life without yet knowing it, and overwhelmed by trouble and terror at the prospect of the long path which lay ahead of me in this life.' At first 'violent passions', as Tocqueville described his youthful liaisons, had helped to distract him from this despair and the 'intellectual ruins' which resulted from this crisis.

Yet neither violent passions, nor the liberal beliefs he painfully acquired later in the 1820s, could always protect him from the return of doubt. He dreaded such moments: 'From time to time these impressions of my early youth (I was then sixteen) take possession of me again; I then see the intellectual world spinning and I am left lost in the universal movement which overturns or shakes all the truths on which I have built my beliefs and my actions.' Altogether, it was a 'sad and frightening sickness' that he endured, one which contributed to the 'agitation without cause and without effect which often spins my soul around erratically, like a wheel which has left its axle' (*OC* XVb. 309).

The intensity of Tocqueville's political beliefs owed much to this religious torment. Yet his correspondence with Madame

Swetchine makes it clear that their intensity had a social source as well. Tocqueville's insistence on the importance of political participation had roots in a fear of social isolation, in the spectre of belonging to a class cut off from the rest of the French nation.

I confess to you . . . that isolation has always frightened me, and that I have always had, in order to be happy or even content, a greater need than is wise, to have around me a certain company and to be able to count on the sympathy of some of my fellows. It is especially to me that the profound remark applies: it is not good to be alone.   (*OC* XVb. 268)

That sense of dependence on others, together with the maxim that all men are brothers, led him to conclude that the only durable basis for any social power is the free concurrence of wills. For that alone turns power into authority. It was because the French *noblesse* had forgotten that truth that they found themselves persecuted after 1789.

For Tocqueville, the Second Empire was doubly a disaster therefore. It not only ran counter to his political beliefs. It left him isolated from his contemporaries. The French educated classes had acquiesced in a tyrannical regime which they did not really consider to be legitimate. For that reason the Second Empire would not survive any major reverses. However, in the meantime, his contemporaries' ideas and sentiments made him feel like an exile. 'You cannot imagine, Madame, how painful and often cruel it is for me to live in this sort of moral isolation', he wrote on 7 January 1857. 'Solitude in the wilderness would often appear to me less hard than this sort of solitude among people' (*OC* XVb. 268).

During the July Monarchy and the Second Republic, he had always felt a particular gratitude to his electors, the gratitude of an aristocrat seeking readmission into French society. Now, alas, he felt compelled to distance himself from that society.

My contemporaries and I are walking along such different routes that we scarcely ever meet one another in the same thoughts and same feelings . . . They have ceased to perceive what still preoccupies me constantly and intensely; they no longer attach importance to the goods to which my heart has remained bound. I have only indifference and sometimes scorn for their new tastes . . . I have relations, neighbours, friends. But my mind no longer has a family or a country. I assure you . . . that this sort of moral and intellectual isolation sometimes gives me a feeling of solitude more intense than any I felt in the American wilderness.   [*OC* XVb. 298]

Class conflict had again led to the loss of political liberty in France. For Tocqueville, who identified so completely with the public weal, it was like the death of a parent or a child.

Epilogue

Alexis de Tocqueville did not leave behind a school of disciples or found an international movement, in the fashion of Karl Marx. Nor did he bequeath to posterity a carefully defined 'scientific' method, in contrast to J. S. Mill, Emile Durkheim, and Max Weber. Fastidious and diffident, Tocqueville drew back from such things. His aristocratic background, joined to the fact that he wrote in the last decades before Western thought became professionally organized, led him to address a wider educated public instead. Tocqueville did not seek merely to interest that public, however. He sought to move the public to act. For, despite his speculative interest in the aristocratic past and the democratic future, everything he wrote was also intensely practical. His major books were political acts, the acts of a citizen.

Perhaps that is why Tocqueville fell into a kind of limbo in the later nineteenth and early twentieth centuries. His writings seemed to elude all categories. His liberalism was not altogether conventional, while his attitude to social theories which claimed scientific status was sceptical, if not downright hostile. Certainly, he detested any social theory which asserted a form of historical determinism. His analysis of the intellectual propensities of a democratic society had alerted him to the way social conditions can foster fatalist forms of social explanation. For 'when all the individual citizens are independent of one another and each is weak, no one can be found exercising very great ... or lasting influence over the masses. At first sight individuals appear to have no influence over them at all, and society would seem to progress on its own by the free and spontaneous movement of all its members' (OC Ib. 89). The first duty, therefore, of anyone writing in a democratic age was to assert and defend the reality of free will. For Tocqueville, it was axiomatic that a people always has the 'faculty of modifying its own lot'.

He had a horror of passivity, of resigned obedience or apolitical scepticism. Such qualities ran against the aristocratic grain in him. They were facets of nineteenth-century bourgeois culture which he could never accept—a culture which had been shaped before citizenship was a real option for the European middle classes. If anything could be salvaged from the aristocratic past and put to the service of the democratic future, it was, Tocqueville believed, the insistence on having a share in power and decision-making. Not to be a citizen, was to be less than a man.

At first glance, Tocqueville's vindication of citizenship might seem to have an entirely classical character. But, in fact, there was a radical divide between the ideas of Aristotle and those of Tocqueville. The ancient Greek conception of citizenship had roots in what Tocqueville called aristocratic social conditions. Inseparable from the appeal of citizenship for the Greeks was the appeal of a superior social rank, one which excluded slaves, women, and the foreign-born. Citizens were a privileged caste, a caste on parade before their inferiors.

Tocqueville's conversion to liberalism—his coming to recognize a deep analogy between Christian morality and the liberal theory of justice—led him to modify that classical conception of citizenship. Denying, up to a point, his own aristocratic tastes, he forged a new conception of and justification for active citizenship, one which was not only open to all adult members of society, but imposed a kind of duty on each. Tocqueville believed that unless that duty was taken seriously, the rights which a liberal society guaranteed would always remain precarious and might even become morally hazardous. They might foster the mere privatizing of life, and with it, contribute to the growth of powerful state machines, a new bureaucratic form of tyranny. The threat which Restoration liberals such as Royer-Collard had alerted him to, would then become only too real. From an 'atomized' society would emerge 'centralization'.

It is often claimed that the theme of bureaucracy first appeared in political thought at the end of the nineteenth century, with the writings of Michels, Mosca, and Weber. But that is untrue. The idea of centralization put forward by Restoration liberals and refined by Tocqueville really marks the entry of the problem of bureaucracy into modern consciousness. It raised new questions about the form of the state, and gave to constitutional theory a different direction and vocabulary—revealing inadequacies previously unnoticed in Montesquieu's theory of the separation of powers in central government. For what guarantee did the formal separation of powers provide against a concentration of powers at the centre—that is, against the destruction of local autonomy? It was that concern which had, by the 1820s, created a new interest in federalism in France, and in the next decade led Tocqueville to write *Democracy in America*. The French state machine, created by Louis XIV and Richelieu, 'perfected' by Napoleon, and inherited by the Restoration, offered a disturbing example. For the extent of central power threatened to make a mockery of all attempts to extend the representative principle to local and regional government.

With the help of the American federalist example, Tocqueville was able to advance beyond Restoration liberalism. He related new constitutional issues to the nature and direction of social change by demonstrating why democratic social conditions require a new model of the state. 'A new political science is needed for a world itself quite new.' Tocqueville used the concept of centralization to identify the need for a new form of the state which 'artificially' protected the local autonomy which had been a 'natural' or built-in feature of aristocratic society in Europe.

In effect, Tocqueville identified a structural flaw in democratic societies—the way societies founded on the principle of civil equality offer no *intrinsic* obstacle to the growth of central power, the power of a state which can alone claim to speak for all equally. In doing so, he remedied a serious weakness of the model of society and government that nineteenth-century liberals had inherited from seventeenth-century Contract Theory, which moved from the 'natural' individual to the association of all, or the state, without making adequate provision for intermediate associations.

But Tocqueville was concerned to explore the moral as well as the political threats resulting from the scale of modern social organization, from a market economy and the nation-state. In his view, the change in scale accompanying the triumph of social equality made the classical idea of citizenship, and with it the whole classical republican idiom, anachronistic and potentially dangerous in the modern world. It did not address the need for a new idea of the state—one which not only made it possible to combine central power with local autonomy, but joined the civil liberties underlying a market economy with the disciplines of political participation. These disciplines help to moralize citizens and limit the privatizing of life. Only in that way could 'individualism', the narrowest economic rationality, be contained in modern democratic societies.

Throughout his life, Tocqueville was preoccupied with the will and the conditions of its exercise. It was, in his view, the human faculty most endangered by democratic social conditions—which, through their influence on the imagination, tend to give men an insignificant idea of what they could achieve by their own exertions. The importance of legitimate self-assertion, of 'virility', runs through his writings. It is the importance for democratic man of not being cowed by his being merely one among so many and of discounting what he can achieve by his own efforts. That false and unnecessary self-abnegation—which can easily become an excuse for pursuing merely private ends—was the moral danger most to be feared in the foreseeable, that is, democratic future.

Here we can begin to detect some of Tocqueville's influence on later thinkers. For despite the limbo into which he was cast in the later nineteenth century because his writings did not fit into new professional categories, Tocqueville's influence was both widespread and profound. Indeed, it can hardly be exaggerated. Few major intellectuals in the hundred years after his death failed to read and ponder over *Democracy in America*.

The most unconventional of them were influenced especially by his account of the threats to the will and human freedom posed by a mass or democratic society. There is a story as yet unwritten about the influence of Tocqueville's analysis on Nietzsche—and on the genesis of the idea of the *Übermensch* in the *Genealogy of Morals*, where Nietzsche relied on aristocratic models to attack a weakening or paralysis of the will in modern democratic societies. The crucial difference, of course, is that Tocqueville's vindication of the will (through his doctrine of citizenship) remained bounded by the moral claims of liberal justice. Tocqueville did not share Nietzsche's contempt for Christianity.

A more widespread form of Tocqueville's influence was on the development of sociological thought. Here Tocqueville benefited from the Great Debate of the Restoration, which had imposed on French liberals the need to preface their political argument with systematic comparison of two types of society, aristocratic and

141

democratic. That comparison had been undertaken in a more rhetorical way by Burke in the 1790s and by Carlyle and Coleridge in the 1820s. It had also loomed large in the denunciations of modernity by French critics of the Revolution such as Joseph de Maistre and Louis de Bonald. But in *Democracy in America* Tocqueville made the comparison with unprecedented subtlety and detachment. He separated more clearly than his predecessors the analytical from the evaluative aspects of the comparison, making it clear that each type of society carried with it advantages and disadvantages. Neither type of society was presented as demonic, neither as a utopia.

The systematic comparison of two types of society, in order to explore the nature of modernity, became a kind of norm after Tocqueville. In that way *Democracy in America* helped to create a new form of self-consciousness, an awareness of the social conditions of our own actions. Among those who learned from Tocqueville in the generation after his death were Frederic le Play, who explored the way larger social changes were reflected in the changing structure of the European family; Ferdinand Tonnies, who reformulated Tocqueville's distinction into one between *Gemeinschaft* and *Gesellschaft* ('community' and 'civil society'); and the Cambridge professor Henry Maine, whose typology held that all societies tend to move from relations governed by status (aristocracy) to relations governed by contract (democracy). Even more striking is the debt of the turn-of-the-century sociologist, Émile Durkheim, to *Democracy in America*. Durkheim's distinction between mechanical solidarity and organic solidarity builds upon Tocqueville's insight into the contrast between, on the one hand, a decentralized society where castes and corporations provided people with strong shared identities, despite their real independence; and, on the other hand, a society where civil equality creates a sense of personal autonomy, despite much greater real dependence on others through the division of labour.

It is when we consider Max Weber in relation to Tocqueville, that the usual account of the development of sociological thought seems most misleading. For Weber has been given credit for insisting that a positivist or causal model for social explanation was inadequate. It had to be supplemented, Weber argued, by imagining typical agents, if the reasons for acting in different types of society were to be understood. That is, both understanding and causal explanation were necessary if sociology was not to be crudely reductionist. But what is striking about Weber's programme is that Tocqueville had already carried it out in *Democracy in America*. Without making a fuss about his method, or claiming that it remedied deficiencies in earlier social thought, Tocqueville had done fifty years before what Weber presented as a programme for the future.

Indeed, Weber's call for social thinkers to combine external or causal explanation with internal understanding of the meaning of action may have owed something to Tocqueville. Usually Weber's recommendations have been seen as a synthesis of Marxist materialism and a German philosophical tradition emphasizing *verstehen* (understanding the meaning of action), but there may be a simpler explanation. Benefiting from developments in early nineteenth-century French philosophy through his study of Guizot's writings, Tocqueville came to rely on typical agents to explore the contrast between aristocratic and democratic societies, placing strong emphasis on the different reasons governing action in each. 'Democratic man' and 'aristocratic man' animate the pages of *Democracy in America* in a highly suggestive way. It is thus possible that Weber was led to his conclusions by Tocqueville's example—for *Democracy in America* was one of the last things Weber read before visiting the United States, and that journey helped to put an end to a fallow period in his writing.

But by far the most tantalizing case is that of Karl Marx. In retrospect, the weakness of Marx's thought is his apparent lack of interest in political organization and theory, which has contributed to the deep crisis in socialist thought in our own day. Yet, paradoxically, Marx's conviction about the political arrangements of a post-revolutionary society—a society which has gone beyond class conflict and in which, on his assumptions, the state could therefore 'wither away'—may have been influenced by a reading of *Democracy in America*. Had Marx been struck by the extent to which American federalism represented a new form of the state, one in which its coercive role was radically reduced? It is possible. We know that Marx spent the year 1843–4 devouring the writings of French liberals such as Guizot, Tocqueville, and Beaumont— writings which introduced him to a sociological mode of thought

143

and helped to break the hold of German metaphysics over him. These 'bourgeois' writings emphasized the importance of class conflict in European history, while Tocqueville relied on the absence of class consciousness in order to explain how Americans had invented a new form of the state and not succumbed to centralization. It may be that Marx began to have something like American federalism in mind for his post-revolutionary order, though of course that order would rest on different property arrangements. If so, Marx may have decided that issues about the form of government could safely be postponed until his own 'scientific' analysis of the course of class conflict had contributed to general insurrection and the victory of the proletariat. 'Democracy' would then, Marx assumed, naturally and effortlessly express itself in decentralized political forms.

The thrust of Tocqueville's writings, however, is that the elimination of social privilege does not *by itself* eliminate the problem of government. There is even a sense in which democratic social conditions, because of the new scale of organization involved, make the problem of government more intractable—more intractable because participation in public decision-making has to be artificially encouraged. The 'natural' inclination of such a society is to a kind of privatizing of life. But are commerce and private friendships enough?

Just as the destruction of a caste society in 1789 had seemed to Restoration liberals to make the state machine inherited from the *ancien régime* redundant, and to open the way to self-government, so Marx assumed that the destruction of a class society (on his special definition of class) opened the way to the disintegration of the state in its centralized, coercive form—and to the true emancipation of individuals. That, however, is the point at which Tocqueville goes beyond both Restoration liberals and Marx. Tocqueville raises new and difficult questions about the fate of citizenship in the modern world, questions which are still pertinent.

Tocqueville draws attention to the impact of the 'democratic revolution' on *mœurs*, to the longer consequences of class conflict during the transition from aristocracy to democracy. In France, such class conflicts had not only created a bureaucratic and potentially tyrannical form of the state. They had also had a disastrous effect on the habits and attitudes underlying the political system. Class hatreds, such as those France had known, destroy the habit of co-operation among a people, and a centralized state, originally the product of class conflict, can keep people apart long after their original grievances disappear. The resulting 'atomization' of society perpetuates centralized power, for people no longer have to co-operate in the management of local affairs. Local government, which ought to act as a 'school for citizens', has given way to local administration, which does nothing to create citizens or civic spirit. Quite the contrary. 'The division of property has lessened the distances which separate the rich from the poor; but it would seem that, the closer they come to each other, the greater is their mutual hatred and the more vehement the envy and the dread with which they resist each other's share in power' (*OC* Ia. 8).

Thus, habits and attitudes born during the transition from aristocracy to democracy may continue to prevent the development of free *mœurs*. When that is so, a democratic society rapidly becomes its own oppressor.

It is hard to see how the state can 'wither away' or power be devolved suddenly in a society where class struggle and the centralization of power have destroyed the habits and even ideas of self-government. In Tocqueville's eyes, the difficulty of establishing representative government in France after 1789 testified to that. The determination to influence public decisions and have a share in power is itself the first victim of administrative centralization. That is why the destruction of aristocracy in France, the only social class which had once had truly free *mœurs*, posed terrible obstacles to the organization of French democracy.

To suppose a change in laws will lead suddenly or inexorably to a change in *mœurs* is utopian and dangerous. For that reason, in *Democracy in America*, Tocqueville insists that while laws are more important than physical circumstances, *mœurs* are more important than laws for the success of free institutions. The implication for liberal thought today is clear. Liberalism cannot afford to concentrate merely on the legal sphere or market relations, on law or the economy. Its primary concern—and the first goal of public policy—must always be the promotion of free *mœurs*. For the quality of the citizenry is the final guarantee of a free society. Forms of liberal thought which obscure that are ultimately self-defeating.

In recent decades liberal thinking about democracy has resulted in the emergence of two schools, almost two armed camps. One school insists that, in a world of nation-states and market economies realism requires that democracy be understood as a method of choosing leaders—a competition between élites or parties understood on the analogy of companies competing for consumer preferences in a market-place. Against that view, which is associated especially with the writings of Joseph Schumpeter, another school has reasserted the importance of participation, drawing on classical ideas and Rousseau's writings to hold up the enlargement of the self and dispersal of power as the point of democracy.

Yet Tocqueville would have seen this as a false dilemma. His notion of free *mœurs* enabled him to cut deeper. For it draws attention to the need to spread as widely as possible in democratic societies the self-confidence and determination which were once the attributes of a privileged class. Such qualities not only help to turn men into citizens—moralizing their intentions as they take up public issues—but also make them better judges of the claims of those who seek to lead them. Constitutional rules can never by themselves guarantee that those who govern will be able and responsible. But, when they are backed by free *mœurs*, that outcome becomes at least more probable.

The argument running through Tocqueville's writings is that self-reliance, the habit of association, and civic spirit can only be created slowly, through a kind of contrivance or artifice, in societies which, like France, have become democratic through bitter class conflict and the concentration of power. Even in societies which are fortunate enough to possess these qualities already, such as Britain and the United States, they must be constantly defended—especially as remedies for injustice often seem to entail administrative centralization. In fact, a decentralized form of the state, which involves people in the management of their own affairs, is indispensable. Constitutional issues and the quality of *mœurs* are to that extent intimately related. And that, rather than any model for exact imitation, is the lesson Tocqueville drew from American federalism. He sought to remind his democratic readers that even after social privilege has been eliminated, the extent of state power and its distribution remain fundamental issues. Democratic legitimacy does not remove the reality of power.

It was an aristocrat's insight.

Suggested reading

A new and exhaustive edition of the works of Tocqueville is nearly, though not quite, complete: *Œuvres, papiers et correspondance d'Alexis de Tocqueville (Œuvres complètes)*, Édition definitive sous la direction de J. P. Mayer et sous le patronage de la Commission nationale (Paris). The first *tome* (in 2 volumes) appeared in 1951. This new edition supersedes the earlier 9 volume edition of Tocqueville's *Œuvres complètes*, ed. Gustave de Beaumont, (Paris, 1861–6). There is an important new critical edition of *Democracy in America*, 2 vols., ed. Edoardo Nolla (Paris, 1990) which includes passages omitted by Tocqueville in the published version as well as comments on his manuscript by family and friends.

Among the most important and useful English translations of Tocqueville's writings are the following:

Democracy in America, translated by George Lawrence and edited by J. P. Mayer and Max Lerner. This translation is on the whole preferable to the original translation by Henry Reeve (even when revised by Francis Bowen).

Journey to America, trans. George Lawrence, ed. J. P. Mayer (New Haven, Conn., 1960).

Journeys to England and Ireland, trans. George Lawrence and J. P. Mayer, ed. J. P. Mayer (London, 1958).

Recollections, trans. George Lawrence, ed. J. P. Mayer and A. P. Kerr (New York, 1968).

The 'Ancien Régime' and the French Revolution, trans. Stuart Gilbert (New York, 1955). There is an even more recent translation by John Bonner, *The 'Ancien Régime'* (London, 1988).

'On the Social and Political Condition of France', *London and Westminster Review* (Apr. 1836), 137–69, trans. John Stuart Mill.

SECONDARY WORKS

Biographical

Here the most important work to date is *Tocqueville* by Andre Jardin (London, 1988). Jardin has done much of the editorial work for the new edition of the *Œuvres complètes*, and the biography benefits especially from his formidable knowledge of the family background and the political history of the period. Less successful is his treatment of the ideas. See also J. P. Mayer's *Prophet of the Mass Ages: A Study of Alexis de Tocqueville* (London, 1949).

Intellectual background

Larry Siedentop, 'Two Liberal Traditions', in *The Idea of Freedom*, ed. A. Ryan (Oxford, 1979); George Armstrong Kelly, *The Human Comedy: Constant, Tocqueville, and French Liberalism* (Cambridge, 1992); Stanley Mellon, *Political Uses of History* (Stanford, Calif., 1958); Pierre Rosanvallon, *Le Moment Guizot* (Paris, 1985).

General studies

Three essays on Tocqueville's thought stand out. John Stuart Mill's 'De Tocqueville's Democracy in America', *London Review* (Oct. 1835); and 'Democracy in America', *Edinburgh Review* (Oct. 1840); Raymond Aron's chapter on 'Tocqueville' in *Main Currents of Sociological Thought* (London, 1965) i. There is also a useful recent collection of essays, *Reconsidering Tocqueville's Democracy in America*, ed. A. Eisenstadt (Rutgers, 1988). Among the more important books are Jack Lively, *The Social and Political Thought of Tocqueville* (Oxford, 1962); Jean Claude Lamberti, *Tocqueville et les deux democraties* (Paris, 1983); Irving Zeitlin, *Liberty, Equality and Revolution in Alexis de Tocqueville* (Boston, 1971); Seymour Drescher, *Dilemmas of Democracy: Tocqueville and Modernization* (Pittsburgh, 1968); R. Pierre Marcel, *Essai politique sur Alexis de Tocqueville* (Paris, 1910); Marvin Zetterbaum, *Tocqueville and the Problem of Democracy* (Stanford, Calif., 1967); Hugh Brogan, *Tocqueville* (London, 1973).

On the American journey and the writing of Democracy in America

Here the magisterial work is George Pierson's, *Tocqueville and Beaumont in America* (New York, 1938). An abridged edition prepared by Dudley Lunt appeared as *Tocqueville in America* (New York, 1959). On the composition of the book the most important study is James Schleifer's *The Making of Tocqueville's Democracy in America* (Chapel Hill, NC, 1980).

On Tocqueville's relations with Britain and the British

Seymour Drescher, *Tocqueville and England* (Cambridge, Mass., 1964).

On the concept of individualism

Jean-Claude Lamberti, *La notion d'individualisme chez Tocqueville* (Paris, 1970); Steven Lukes, *Individualism* (Oxford, 1973).

Suggested reading

On Tocqueville during the July Monarchy

Mary Lawlor, *Alexis de Tocqueville in the Chamber of Deputies: His Views on Foreign and Colonial Policy* (Washington, 1959); Seymour Drescher (ed.), *Tocqueville and Beaumont on Social Reform* (New York, 1968).

On Tocqueville and religion

Doris Goldstein, *Trial of Faith: Religion and Politics in Tocqueville's Thought* (New York, 1975).

On the writing of The Ancien Régime *and the Revolution*

Richard Herr, *Tocqueville and the Old Regime* (Princeton, NJ, 1962).

On Tocqueville's intellectual legacy

Here the works which might be cited are legion, but among the most interesting are: Louis Dumont, *Homo Hierarchicus* (London, 1970); David Riesman, *The Lonely Crowd* (New Haven, 1950); James Bryce, *The American Commonwealth* (London, 1888); Louis Hartz, *The Liberal Tradition in America* (New York, 1955); Robert Dahl, *A Preface to Democratic Theory* (Chicago, 1956).

Index

OXFORD

MORE OXFORD PAPERBACKS

This book is just one of nearly 1000 Oxford Paperbacks currently in print. If you would like details of other Oxford Paperbacks, including titles in the World's Classics, Oxford Reference, Oxford Books, OPUS, Past Masters, Oxford Authors, and Oxford Shakespeare series, please write to:

UK and Europe: Oxford Paperbacks Publicity Manager, Arts and Reference Publicity Department, Oxford University Press, Walton Street, Oxford OX2 6DP.

Customers in UK and Europe will find Oxford Paperbacks available in all good bookshops. But in case of difficulty please send orders to the Cash-with-Order Department, Oxford University Press Distribution Services, Saxon Way West, Corby, Northants NN18 9ES. Tel: 0536 741519; Fax: 0536 746337. Please send a cheque for the total cost of the books, plus £1.75 postage and packing for orders under £20; £2.75 for orders over £20. Customers outside the UK should add 10% of the cost of the books for postage and packing.

USA: Oxford Paperbacks Marketing Manager, Oxford University Press, Inc., 200 Madison Avenue, New York, N.Y. 10016.

Canada: Trade Department, Oxford University Press, 70 Wynford Drive, Don Mills, Ontario M3C 1J9.

Australia: Trade Marketing Manager, Oxford University Press, G.P.O. Box 2784Y, Melbourne 3001, Victoria.

South Africa: Oxford University Press, P.O. Box 1141, Cape Town 8000.

PAST MASTERS

General Editor: Keith Thomas

Past Masters is a series of authoritative studies that introduce students and general readers alike to the thought of leading intellectual figures of the past whose ideas still influence many aspects of modern life.

'This Oxford University Press series continues on its encyclopaedic way ... One begins to wonder whether any intelligent person can afford not to possess the whole series.' *Expository Times*

KIERKEGAARD

Patrick Gardiner

Søren Kierkegaard (1813–55), one of the most original thinkers of the nineteenth century, wrote widely on religious, philosophical, and literary themes. But his idiosyncratic manner of presenting some of his leading ideas initially obscured their fundamental import.

This book shows how Kierkegaard developed his views in emphatic opposition to prevailing opinions, including certain metaphysical claims about the relation of thought to existence. It describes his reaction to the ethical and religious theories of Kant and Hegel, and it also contrasts his position with doctrines currently being advanced by men like Feuerbach and Marx. Kierkegaard's seminal diagnosis of the human condition, which emphasizes the significance of individual choice, has arguably been his most striking philosophical legacy, particularly for the growth of existentialism. Both that and his arresting but paradoxical conception of religious belief are critically discussed, Patrick Gardiner concluding this lucid introduction by indicating salient ways in which they have impinged on contemporary thought.

Also available in Past Masters:

PAST MASTERS

General Editor: Keith Thomas

The *Past Masters* series offers students and general readers alike concise introductions to the lives and works of the world's greatest literary figures, composers, philosophers, religious leaders, scientists, and social and political thinkers.

'Put end to end, this series will constitute a noble encyclopaedia of the history of ideas.' Mary Warnock

HOBBES

Richard Tuck

Thomas Hobbes (1588–1679) was the first great English political philosopher, and his book *Leviathan* was one of the first truly modern works of philosophy. He has long had the reputation of being a pessimistic atheist, who saw human nature as inevitably evil, and who proposed a totalitarian state to subdue human failings. In this new study, Richard Tuck shows that while Hobbes may indeed have been an atheist, he was far from pessimistic about human nature, nor did he advocate totalitarianism. By locating him against the context of his age, Dr Tuck reveals Hobbs to have been passionately concerned with the refutation of scepticism in both science and ethics, and to have developed a theory of knowledge which rivalled that of Descartes in its importance for the formation of modern philosophy.

Also available in Past Masters:

PAST MASTERS

General Editor: Keith Thomas

The people whose ideas have made history . . .

'One begins to wonder whether any intelligent person can afford not to possess the whole series.' *Expository Times*

JESUS

Humphrey Carpenter

Jesus wrote no books, but the influence of his life and teaching has been immeasurable. Humphrey Carpenter's account of Jesus is written from the standpoint of an historian coming fresh to the subject without religious preconceptions. And no previous knowledge of Jesus or the Bible on the reader's part is assumed.

How reliable are the Christian 'Gospels' as an account of what Jesus did or said? How different were his ideas from those of his contemporaries? What did Jesus think of himself? Humphrey Carpenter begins his answer to these questions with a survey and evaluation of the evidence on which our knowledge of Jesus is based. He then examines his teaching in some detail, and reveals the perhaps unexpected way in which his message can be said to be original. In conclusion he asks to what extent Jesus's teaching has been followed by the Christian Churches that have claimed to represent him since his death.

'Carpenter's *Jesus* is about as objective as possible, while giving every justifiable emphasis to the real and persistent forcefulness of the moral teaching of this charismatic personality.' Kathleen Nott, *The Times*

'an excellent, straightforward presentation of up-to-date scholarship' David L. Edwards, *Church Times*

Also available in Past Masters:

Muhammad Michael Cook
Aquinas Anthony Kenny
Cervantes P. E. Russell
Clausewitz Michael Howard

PAST MASTERS

General Editor: Keith Thomas

Past Masters is a series of concise, lucid, and authoritative introductions to the thought of leading intellectual figures of the past whose ideas still affect the way we think today.

'One begins to wonder whether any intelligent person can afford not to possess the whole series.' *Expository Times*

FREUD

Anthony Storr

Sigmund Freud (1865–1939) revolutionized the way in which we think about ourselves. From its beginnings as a theory of neurosis, Freud developed psycho-analysis into a general psychology which became widely accepted as the predominant mode of discussing personality and interpersonal relationships.

From its inception, the psycho-analytic movement has always aroused controversy. Some have accepted Freud's views uncritically: others have dismissed psycho-analysis as unscientific without appreciating its positive contributions. Fifty years have passed since Freud's death, so it is now possible to assess his ideas objectively. Anthony Storr, psychotherapist and writer, takes a new, critical look at Freud's major theories and at Freud himself in a book which both specialists and newcomers to Freud's work will find refreshing.

Also available in Past Masters:

OPUS

General Editors: Walter Bodmer, Christopher Butler, Robert Evans, John Skorupski

A HISTORY OF WESTERN PHILOSOPHY

This series of OPUS books offers a comprehensive and up-to-date survey of the history of philosophical ideas from earliest times. Its aim is not only to set those ideas in their immediate cultural context, but also to focus on their value and relevance to twentieth-century thinking.

CLASSICAL THOUGHT

Terence Irwin

Spanning over a thousand years from Homer to Saint Augustine, *Classical Thought* encompasses a vast range of material, in succinct style, while remaining clear and lucid even to those with no philosophical or Classical background.

The major philosophers and philosophical schools are examined—the Presocratics, Socrates, Plato, Aristotle, Stoicism, Epicureanism, Neoplatonism; but other important thinkers, such as Greek tragedians, historians, medical writers, and early Christian writers, are also discussed. The emphasis is naturally on questions of philosophical interest (although the literary and historical background to Classical philosophy is not ignored), and again the scope is broad—ethics, the theory of knowledge, philosophy of mind, philosophical theology. All this is presented in a fully integrated, highly readable text which covers many of the most important areas of ancient thought and in which stress is laid on the variety and continuity of philosophical thinking after Aristotle.

Also available in the History of Western Philosophy series:

The Rationalists John Cottingham
Continental Philosophy since 1750 Robert C. Solomon
The Empiricists R. S. Woolhouse

PHILOSOPHY IN OXFORD PAPERBACKS

Ranging from authoritative introductions in the Past Masters and OPUS series to in-depth studies of classical and modern thought, the Oxford Paperbacks' philosophy list is one of the most provocative and challenging available.

THE GREAT PHILOSOPHERS

Bryan Magee

Beginning with the death of Socrates in 399, and following the story through the centuries to recent figures such as Bertrand Russell and Wittgenstein, Bryan Magee and fifteen contemporary writers and philosophers provide an accessible and exciting introduction to Western philosophy and its greatest thinkers.

Bryan Magee in conversation with:

A. J. Ayer	John Passmore
Michael Ayers	Anthony Quinton
Miles Burnyeat	John Searle
Frederick Copleston	Peter Singer
Hubert Dreyfus	J. P. Stern
Anthony Kenny	Geoffrey Warnock
Sidney Morgenbesser	Bernard Williams
Martha Nussbaum	

'Magee is to be congratulated . . . anyone who sees the programmes or reads the book will be left in no danger of believing philosophical thinking is unpractical and uninteresting.' Ronald Hayman, *Times Educational Supplement*

'one of the liveliest, fast-paced introductions to philosophy, ancient and modern that one could wish for' *Universe*

Also by Bryan Magee in Oxford Paperbacks:

Men of Ideas
Aspects of Wagner 2/e

RELIGION AND THEOLOGY
IN OXFORD PAPERBACKS

Oxford Paperbacks offers incisive studies of the philosophies and ceremonies of the world's major religions,
including Christianity, Judaism, Islam, Buddhism, and
Hinduism.

A HISTORY OF HERESY

David Christie-Murray

'Heresy, a cynic might say, is the opinion held by a minority of
men which the majority declares unacceptable and is strong
enough to punish.'

What is heresy? Who were the great heretics and what did they
believe? Why might those originally condemned as heretics
come to be regarded as martyrs and cherished as saints?

Heretics, those who dissent from orthodox Christian belief,
have existed at all times since the Christian Church was founded
and the first Christians became themselves heretics within
Judaism. From earliest times too, politics, orthodoxy, and
heresy have been inextricably entwined—to be a heretic was
often to be a traitor and punishable by death at the stake—and
heresy deserves to be placed against the background of political
and social developments which shaped it.

This book is a vivid combination of narrative and comment
which succeeds in both re-creating historical events and elu-
cidating the most important—and most disputed—doctrines
and philosophies.

Also in Oxford Paperbacks:

Christianity in the West 1400–1700   John Bossy
John Henry Newman: A Biography   Ian Ker
Islam: The Straight Path   John L. Esposito

HISTORY IN OXFORD PAPERBACKS

Oxford Paperbacks offers a comprehensive list of books on British history, ranging from Frank Stenton's *Anglo-Saxon England* to John Guy's *Tudor England*, and from Christopher Hill's *A Turbulent, Seditious, and Factious People* to Kenneth O. Morgan's *Labour in Power: 1945– 1951*.

TUDOR ENGLAND
John Guy

Tudor England is a compelling account of political and religious developments from the advent of the Tudors in the 1460s to the death of Elizabeth I in 1603.

Following Henry VII's capture of the Crown at Bosworth in 1485, Tudor England witnessed far-reaching changes in government and the Reformation of the Church under Henry VIII, Edward VI, Mary, and Elizabeth; that story is enriched here with character studies of the monarchs and politicians that bring to life their personalities as well as their policies.

Authoritative, clearly argued, and crisply written, this comprehensive book will be indispensable to anyone interested in the Tudor Age.

'lucid, scholarly, remarkably accomplished . . . an excellent overview' *Sunday Times*

'the first comprehensive history of Tudor England for more than thirty years' Patrick Collinson, *Observer*

Also in Oxford Paperbacks:

John Calvin   William J. Bouwsma
Early Modern France 1515–1715   Robin Briggs
The Spanish Armada   Felipe Fernández-Armesto
Time in History   G. J. Whitrow